SE...

Serbi...
English–Serbian
Dictionary
&
Phrasebook

by
Nicholas Awde
&
Duška Radosavljević

HIPPOCRENE BOOKS INC
New York

**Thanks to Nicholas Williams and Robert Stanley Martin
for their help in compiling this volume.**

———◆———

Typeset & designed by Desert♥Hearts

ISBN 0-7818-1049-3

For information, address:
HIPPOCRENE BOOKS, INC.
171 Madison Avenue
New York, NY 10016
www.hippocrenebooks.com

Printed in the United States of America

CONTENTS

- A Serb man is a **Srbin**.
- A Serb woman is a **Srpkinja**.
- The adjective Serbian is **srpski**.
- Serbians call themselves **Srbi.**
- The Serbian language is **srpski jezik**.

INTRODUCTION

Serbian as a language is part of what is known as Serbo-Croatian, the language of the Former Yugoslavia. It was standardized in the nineteenth century from the major dialects spoken in the region by the Serbian language reformer Vuk Karadžić and the Croatian Ljudevit Gaj. This became the basis of the standard literary Serbo-Croatian language.

Following the disintegration of Yugoslavia, the language spoken in Croatia became known as Croatian, the language spoken in Bosnia as Bosnian and the language spoken in Serbia and Montenegro as Serbian. All three languages have attempted to reconstruct their vocabulary in order to differentiate themselves from Serbo-Croatian.

Early history

The recorded history of the territory covered by the former Yugoslavia dates back to the seventh century BC, when the ancient Greeks were trading and creating colonies along the Adriatic coast and the Balkan territories, which were then inhabited by Illyrian and Thracian tribes. However, archaeological findings in the area have revealed evidence of civilizations dating back at least to the Bronze Age. Sites in Croatia — Istra and Hvar — date back to 4000 BC, while a site excavated in 1965 in Lepenski Vir, which is on the River Danube in eastern Serbia, dates back to 6000 BC.

Around the third century BC, Celtic tribes migrated to the east of the Balkans. At the time, the Macedonian Empire spread through the south of the region and the Roman Empire soon began to expand eastwards from across the Adriatic. The tensions between various tribes and empires continued for several centuries. Roman sites still survive throughout this area, most notably in Dalmatia and Istria, both in Croatia.

The division of the Roman Empire into Rome and Byzantium in 285 AD had a direct effect on the future of the Balkans. The dividing line ran across Montenegro, Bosnia, and Serbia, resulting in the development of distinct cultures on either side of the line, a development that still shows its influence today.

Driven by the raids of Barbarian tribes, the Slavs migrated southwards from the Carpathian Mountains, settleing in the Balkan semi-peninsula around the seventh century AD. They arrived in three groups: the Slovenes and Croats inhabited the northern and western regions respectively, and the Serbs settled to the south of the Danube, on the eastern side of the border between Rome and Byzantium.

The first kingdoms

Originally the three Slav groups shared the same language and cultural identity. However, over the centuries they developed distinct cultural and linguistic features. The region that the Slovenes inhabited was mostly under Germanic rule and, in the sixteenth century, the region was incorporated into the Habsburg Empire, based in Austria. In spite of this, the Slovenes retained their Slavic cultural identity.

The Croats created their first kingdom under King Tomislav in 924, which lasted until 1089 when they fell under Hungarian rule. However, Dalmatia — part of present-day Croatia and Italy — had a different cultural genesis. Originally inhabited by Greeks and Romans, it consequently fell under the control of various powers, but its strongest influence came from Venice, as epitomized by Dubrovnik — one of the most renowned Venetian city-states. Venetian rule lasted from the thirteenth century until the Napoleonic conquest in 1797, when the region was named the Illyrian Province. Following a brief French occupation, Dalmatia eventually came under Austrian (Habsburg) rule.

The territory of today's Bosnia-Herzegovina was originally part of the medieval Hungarian empire until 1180, when it became an independent kingdom under Kulin Ban. The new realm was characterized by its adoption of the heretical Christianity preached by the Bogomils, who believed in a spiritual church in which all believers had an equal share. By the late fourteenth century, Bosnia had expanded into Serbia and Dalmatia, and become a powerful force in the region under its king, Stefan Tvrtko.

But after Bosnia came under the control of the Ottoman Empire in the fifteenth century, much of the Bosnian population converted to Islam for pragmatic reasons.

The Golden Age

Following their arrival in the Balkans, the Serbs organized themselves into communities led by chiefs or *župans*. Struggling against the domination of the Byzantine Empire, by the twelfth century Serbia had emerged as a powerful kingdom under King Stefan Nemanja, who extended his control over Montenegro and parts of present-day Albania.

Stefan Nemanja's eldest son, Rastko, opted for the life of a monk at a monastery on Mount Athos in Greece, where he was renamed Sava and later made a saint. He established the Serbian Orthodox Church in 1219 and built a number of churches in Serbia as well as a Serbian monastery on Mount Athos in Greece.

By the mid-fourteenth century, Serbia had become the most powerful kingdom in the Balkans under the rule of Stefan Dušan Nemanjić. This was Serbia's Golden Age where culture and commerce flourished.

But it was not to last. In 1389, the last Serbian prince, Lazar, led the Serbian army against the mighty Ottoman Empire in a great battle of resistance that became known as the Battle of Kosovo. Prince Lazar and the cream of the Serbian nobility all died heroically in the battle, defeated by the Ottomans.

By 1459, all of Serbia had fallen under Ottoman rule. This sparked great Serbian migrations to Dalmatia, Montenegro, Bosnia, and the Hungarian-controlled region of Vojvodina.

This Golden Age has often been used as a powerful rhetorical device in contemporary times to evoke the people's spirit by the nationalist Serbian politicians of the 1990s. President Slobodan Milošević, for example, rose to power by addressing the Serbian question at the 600th anniversary of the Battle of Kosovo in 1989.

Century of revolt

By the nineteenth century, the Ottoman Empire was beginning to slowly crumble both internally as well as under external pressure from the more powerful nations of Europe, who were ever eager to expand eastwards. The first Serbian uprising against the Ottomans, led by Karadjordje ("Black George") Petrović in 1804 was unsuccessful, although it is considered a turning point in Serbian history.

Initially supported by Russian troops, the revolt escalated, and failed again when Russia withdrew in order to resist the ill-fated invasion by the armies of France's Napoleon. Karadjordje fled to Austria and his role as the leader of the Serbians was taken over by his friend Miloš Obrenović, who proved more skilled at diplomatic negotiations with the Ottomans for Serbian independence.

These two leaders became founders of two ruling dynasties of the new, independent Serbia. The rule of the first, Obrenović dynasty ended with a coup in 1903, after which Karadjordje's descendant, Petar Karadjordjević, ascended the throne.

Balkan independence

Montenegro had emerged as an identifiable geographical and political unit after the Battle of Kosovo. Its mountainous terrain proved an obstacle to Ottoman advances (Montenegro means "Black

Mountain"). By the end of the fifteenth century, a Montenegrin resistance leader Ivan Crnojević formed an independent province with its capital in Cetinje. This later became the seat of the Montenegrin dynasty Petrović, originating from a succession of bishop-kings.

The most famous Montenegrin bishop-king was Petar Petrović Njegoš (1830–50). He was also a poet who created some of the greatest masterpieces of Yugoslav literature, *Gorski Vijenac* (*The Mountain Wreath*) and *Luča Mikrokozma* (*The Light of Microcosm*).

After the Ottoman Empire lost control of the region, Montenegro became sovereign and gained access to the Adriatic Coast at the Congress of Berlin in 1878. The rule of the Petrović dynasty ended in 1916 when the last Montenegrin king, Nikola, fled into exile after a 58-year reign.

The Former Yugoslav Republic of Macedonia, in the southeast of the region, was initially controlled by Byzantium, and also briefly by Bulgarians. In the fourteenth century it became part of the Serbian Empire. Since the Ottoman invasion in the mid-fifteenth century, the region had remained under Ottoman control until the Balkan Wars of 1912–13.

Consequently, the Greeks, Bulgarians and Serbs, having all laid claims to this territory, divided it into three parts, as outlined in the Treaty of Bucharest, in 1913. Macedonia — the name officially accepted after the Second World War when it became a republic within Yugoslavia — has caused problems with neighboring Greece due to that country's northern region, also called Macedonia, which borders with the republic.

Forging an identity

The European Age of Enlightenment began to make its impact in the Balkan region in the early nineteenth century, resulting in increased cultural activity at every level of society. This is when the first theaters, libraries and other cultural institutions opened in Serbia. At the same time, Vuk Stefanović Karadžić, a linguist, ethnographer and cultural activist, undertook the reformation of the Serbian written language on the basis of his research into the spoken language in the linguistic territory covered by Serbo-Croatian.

He consequently dispensed with the official, antiquated Cyrillic script of the Orthodox Church that was officially used and created a phonetic version, more accessible to the masses. The new alphabet, also Cyrillic, had thirty letters, one for each sound, and corresponded with the rule: "Write as you speak, read as it is written."

Following the advice and encouragement of the Slovenian scholar Jernej Kopitar, Vuk Karadžić also collected and recorded Serbian national poetry and prose. These oral epics were, at the same time, historical records of various events, passed down from generation to generation, and delivered to the accompaniment of the national string instrument — the *gusle*.

On his travels to Vienna, Karadžić met the German poet Goethe, who then translated the Serbian epic *Hasanaginica* into German. This is also the period when the cosmopolitan Montenegrin bishop-prince Njegoš wrote the *Mountain Wreath*, and the Croatian linguist Ljudevit Gaj, leader of the pan-Slavic "Illyrian movement," joined efforts with Karadžić to standardize written Croatian and lay the foundations for the Serbo-Croatian language.

Building the kingdom

On the grounds of the cultural and linguistic similarities that the South Slavs shared, by the end of the nineteenth century they were more than receptive to the pan-Slavic movement that was swiftly coinciding with and aiding in the gradual liberation of Slavic regions within Ottoman and Austro-Hungarian Empires.

However, the strength of the movement varied from region to region. Newly liberated Serbia and Montenegro were enthusiastic about unification with their fellow Slavs to the West, the Croatians and Slovenians. The Slovenians under Austrian jurisdiction and Croatians under Hungarian rule were divided among themselves as to whether they wanted sole independence or union with the rest of the South Slavs.

After the withdrawal of the Ottomans, Bosnia was annexed by Austria in 1908, and this is when the pan-Slavic nationalist movement was particularly strong. The hostility to Austro-Hungarian domination, coupled with the movement for independence, led to the fateful shooting of the Austrian archduke Franz Ferdinand. On June 28, 1914, he had chosen to visit Sarajevo on the holiday that marked the anniversary of the Serbian defeat at Kosovo. His assassination there led to the Austrian declaration of war on Serbia and, consequently, to the devastation of the First World War.

By this time, Serbia was a kingdom, the dynasty of Karadjordjević having succeeded the dynasty of Obrenović, following a military coup in 1903 when the unpopular king Aleksandar Obrenović and his mistress were killed. Petar Karadjordjević returned from exile in Geneva, where he had maintained links with the Montenegrin and Russian royal families. On ascending the Serbian throne, he became a benevolent and popular king.

In 1909 he passed over his firstborn son Djordje as heir in favor of his younger son, Aleksandar, who had displayed a greater degree of self-restraint, responsibility and a more serious interest in the affairs of the state.

Aftermath of war

The First World War took Serbia unawares. Having just recovered from the Balkan Wars, the country was not yet ready for another battle. The Austrians invaded in

1914 and, though the Serbian army resisted fiercely, a second attack was stronger and more successful. A combination of the Austrian army, bitter weather conditions and an outbreak of typhoid fever drove the Serbs into retreat.

The new king Aleksandar led his battered army on foot southwards across the mountains of Albania to the Ionian Sea where they were shipped to safety by the Allied powers. At once, Serbian and Croatian politicians abroad lobbied the Allies for the creation of a united South Slavic state following the end of the war.

When hostilities finally ended in 1918, the American president Woodrow Wilson declared his support for the independence of the Slavic regions from Austria-Hungary. The Kingdom of Serbs, Croats and Slovenes, including Montenegro and Bosnia, was created on December 1, 1918.

A united nation

In 1928, the Kingdom of Serbs, Croats and Slovenes was renamed Yugoslavia — meaning "Land of the South Slavs." Headed by the Serbian Aleksandar, the kingdom was seen by other co-nationals, especially the Croats, as a means of Serbian domination.

In spite of the king's efforts to please all the constituent nations — he even considered making official the Roman alphabet (as used by the Croats) at the expense of Serbian Cyrillic — Croatian resistance caused political tension and anarchy in Parliament, which then led to its dissolution and the establishment of direct rule under the king.

King Aleksandar's assassination in Marseilles in 1934 left the country in political turmoil, reflecting the unrest in the rest of Europe as the Second World War approached. The Serbian heir to the throne was too young to take power, and authority passed to the king's cousin and friend from childhood, Regent Pavle (also referred to as Prince Paul).

Meanwhile, in the 1920s, the Yugoslavian

Communist Party had been founded. Its membership consisted largely of the developing working classes and peasants from all over the country. At first the party gained considerable support in both the Serbian capital of Belgrade and the Croatian capital of Zagreb. However, its activism and growing popularity meant that the Communist Party soon found itself banned by the national government and forced underground, where it worked to establish closer links with the Soviet Union. In 1937, Josip Broz Tito was elected the party's general secretary.

When the Second World War started, Yugoslavia proclaimed itself neutral in the conflict. By 1941, however, the Italian-German Axis had forced Prince Paul into an official alliance. This caused a military coup and popular rebellion. Consequently, Belgrade was bombed on April 6, 1941, followed immediately with an invasion by Axis forces. After a brief and unsuccessful military resistance, the country was occupied. Germany annexed Slovenia, Italy took Montenegro and the Adriatic Coast, and Bulgaria took Macedonia.

Serbia remained a puppet state and so did Croatia and Bosnia — both of which were controlled by German-appointed Ante Pavelić, the leader of the Croatian pro-Nazi faction, the Ustaše. A great number of atrocities were committed during this period, including not only the mass deportation and killing of Balkan Jews and Roma (Gypsies) but also Slavic nationalities.

Civil war

The invasions of the Second World War sparked a war of resistance in Yugoslavia not only against the Germans and Italians but also against the pro-Nazi Yugoslavians. In effect the situation had become a complex, terrible civil war. The royal family fled to Britain, while the Royalist Army — known as the Četniks — fought against both the Germans and the

Communist Partisans. The Partisans, led by Tito, finally gained international support at the expense of the Četniks, who were initially supported by the Allies.

Building a power base in his mountain strongholds meant that Tito was eventually able to wrest control of the country, and by 1943 he had already established his own government and formed the People's Federal Republic of Yugoslavia — later renamed the Socialist Federal Republic of Yugoslavia when peace arrived in Europe.

The war's end saw the country emerge with immense losses at every level — an estimated one-tenth of the population lost their lives. However, its borders remained more or less the same, neighboring Italy to the west, Austria and Hungary to the north, Romania and Bulgaria to the east, Greece to the southeast, and Albania to the south.

The transition from monarchy to republic had its own cost. Tito's Communists quickly imposed their authority through as much intimidation as their predecessors had used. Private property was confiscated, and those dubbed "enemies of the people" were tried in court or executed.

Yugoslavia initially followed the Soviet model of governmental organization. However, in 1948 it was expelled from the Comintern — the bloc of Communist nations that were politically and economically controlled by the Soviet Union. Tito's response was simple: he disassociated himself from Stalin and developed his own national and international policies.

The result was a uniquely Yugoslavian brand of socialism based on the principle of "self-management," whereby people were encouraged to run their own farms or companies and profit from this. Such empowerment was clearly at odds with the total state control practised by other Communist countries.

The Tito era

In the 1950s, Tito joined India's Jawarlal Nehru and

Egypt's Gamal Abdel Nasser to form the Non-Aligned Movement, by which Yugoslavia became the only Eastern European country not involved in the Cold War.

However, internal problems remained since Tito was unable to totally eliminate the various movements of unofficial political opposition. He took a hard line with Yugoslav supporters of Stalin and the Soviet Union, for example, and these were imprisoned on the notorious Goli Otok ("Bare Island"), where they underwent ideological re-education under harsh conditions.

Crackdowns on dissenters continued until the early 1950s, but from this period on, a more liberal current gradually emerged within the Yugoslav League of Communists, a phenomenon that Tito quietly tolerated and even at times supported. The 1960s were marked by thriving economic development, which in the 1970s led to a strengthening movement for greater economic and political autonomy of the richer republics, particularly Croatia and Slovenia.

A new constitution in 1974 contributed towards this "devolution" as it allowed for greater decentralization and increased autonomy of the individual republics. Accordingly, two historically distinct areas within Serbia itself — Vojvodina to the north and Kosovo to the south — were also given the status of autonomous regions.

Since 1974, therefore, the Socialist Federal Republic of Yugoslavia consisted of six republics and two autonomous provinces within Serbia, the largest of the republics. Apart from the six major nations in each republic, there were many national minorities living in Yugoslavia, including Albanians, Hungarians, Romanians, Slovaks, Roma, Turks, Italians, and Germans.

The most important policy of the Socialist Yugoslavia was equality and the "brotherhood and unity" of all peoples living in the country. This was reflected in all federal and republic institutions that always endeavored to include representatives from all ethnic groups. These groups had the right to official education, culture and the media in their own language, and a right to practice their own religion, although religion as such was not encouraged by socialism. Nevertheless the socialist years saw a considerable degree of intermarriage between the various religious and ethnic groups, particularly in Bosnia where an impressive ethnic mix coincided with a strong socialist allegiance.

Yugoslavia splits

Following Tito's death in 1980, a series of economic crises hit Yugoslavia. By the early 1980s, ethnic problems resurfaced as a result of this turmoil, with individual republics pushing for ever greater autonomy and individual ethnic groups pushing for more recognition.

The wealthier republics felt disadvantaged at having to finance the poorer ones; the Serbs, dispersed by Communist geographical reorganization, saw themselves as threatened. The Serbs in Kosovo especially feared an increasingly violent Albanian movement for Kosovo independence. The tension finally culminated with a formation of various nationalist movements within the country.

Slovenia was the first to break away, its independence declared with relative ease. Meanwhile, in Serbia, the Serbian nationalist Slobodan Milošević rose to power by withdrawing autonomy from Kosovo and Vojvodina that had been granted to them in 1974. His Croatian counterpart, Franjo Tudjman, won his republic's elections soon after and pressed for Croatian secession from Yugoslavia. But the existence of a considerable Serbian population in Croatia made Croatian secession problematic. Similarly the wide ethnic mix of Bosnia made Bosnian secession even more complicated. All these tensions led finally to the most terrible war in Europe since the Second World War.

Looking to the future

The 1995 Dayton Peace Agreement ended the war in Bosnia, but Milošević's troubles at home continued. Having lost the local elections in 1996, Milošević attempted to annul the results, bringing the increasingly discontented and impoverished people of Serbia out into the streets.

The peaceful student-led demonstrations quickly increased in number, team spirit and good humor, continuing daily for three months in winter 1996-97. The opposition finally gained their seats, but their coalition disintegrated quickly, effectively leaving Milošević still in power. In his last bid to secure his position by diverting public attention to "outside enemies," Milošević turned to the Kosovo problem. This had been simmering ever since his rise to power ten years previously.

Increased activity of the Albanian separatist organization — the Kosovo Liberation Army (K.L.A.) — and frequent clashes between the Serbian Police and the K.L.A. provoked direct international involvement from the N.A.T.O. powers of Western Europe. Unsuccessful negotiations over the future of Kosovo finally led to the thoroughly devastating N.A.T.O. bombing of Yugoslavia in 1999.

Milošević's dictatorship ended on October 5, 2000, following a general election and the brief "Bulldozer Revolution." This marked a turning point in the history of the region, ushering in a democratic government intended to open new horizons and end the post-socialist violence and corruption. As such, Yugoslavia has also begun a period of re-integration within the wider context of Europe, although tensions continue to simmer in Kosovo.

At the time of writing, the Federal Republic of Yugoslavia is called Serbia and Montenegro (**Srbija i Crna Gora**), and negotiations regarding the nature of the federation are in process. ∎

A VERY BASIC GRAMMAR

Serbian belongs to the Slavonic branch of the Indo-European family of languages. Other members of this branch include Croatian, Slovenian, Macedonian and Bulgarian, while relatives in the family include Czech, Slovak, Polish, Ukranian, Byelorussian, and Russian, and, more distantly, English, German, French, Italian, Spanish, Farsi, and Hindi/Urdu. Serbian is spoken in the territories of the Former Yugoslavia. Together with the closely related Croatian, which is spoken in neighboring Croatia, it is also called Serbo-Croat or Serbo-Croatian.

The Slavonic languages all originated from the same language, which in the course of history developed into distinct linguistic units. Along with Croatian and Slovenian, Serbian belongs to the Western South Slavonic unit while Macedonian and Bulgarian belong to the Eastern South Slavonic unit. Eastern South Slavonic also includes the first literary Slavonic language, which dates from the ninth century AD — Old Slavonic, which is based on a Macedonian dialect spoken in the region of Salonica. Old Slavonic is now a dead language, but it formed a basis for the development of other literary languages in the South Slavonic group.

Serbo-Croat can be written in both the Latin and Cyrillic alphabets. The Latin alphabet is used in the western parts of the Former Yugoslavia, such as Croatia and Slovenia, while Cyrillic is used in Serbia, Montenegro and exclusively in the Republic of Macedonia. The order of letters in the two alphabets is different. The Latin alphabet, based on the Western model, is called **"abeceda"** (see page 29), and the

c = hi*ts*   č = *ch*urch   ć = *ty/chy*   đ = *dy*   dž = *jam*

Cyrillic, based on the Greek model, is called **"azbuka"** (see page 32). There are thirty letters in both alphabets, and each letter corresponds to a particular sound. Serbian is a phonetic language and very easy to read.

—Structure

Like English, the linguistic structure of Serbian is basically a simple one. Word order is flexible, e.g.

Ja sam doktor. "I am a doctor."

You can also say:

Doktor sam. "I am a doctor." (literally: "Doctor am.")

—Nouns

Serbian has no words for "the", "a" or "an" in the same way as English does — instead the meaning is generally understood from the context, e.g. **grad** can mean "the town", "a town" or just simply "town."

GENDER — As with many other languages, like German and Russian (and Latin!), Serbian divides words according to gender, i.e. whether they are masculine, feminine or neuter. As a very general rule, masculine nouns end in a consonant, feminine in **-a**, and most neuter nouns end in **-o** or **-e**.

Sometimes gender is predictable: e.g. **čovek** "man", **sin** "son", **telefon** "telephone" (masculine); **žena** "woman", **ćerka** "daughter", **škola** "school" (feminine); and **drvo** "tree", **kilo** "kilogram", **glasanje** "voting" (neuter). Sometimes it is not, e.g. **radio** "radio" (masculine), **jesen** "autumn" (feminine), and **dete** "child" (neuter — remember that a child can be "it" in English too without causing offense!).

Adjectives agree according to gender and take similar forms, e.g.

Masculine: **Moj sin je <u>srećan</u>.**
"My son is happy."
<u>novi</u> telefon
"new telephone"

Feminine: **<u>Moja</u> ćerka je <u>srećna</u>.**
"My daughter is happy."
<u>nova</u> škola
"new school"

Neuter: **<u>Moje</u> dete je <u>srećno</u>.**
"My child is happy."
<u>novo</u> vino
"new wine"

PLURALS — There are a variety of forms for the plural in Serbian; these are sometimes predictable, sometimes not. Some involve a simple change of ending, e.g.

žena "woman" → **žene** "women"
hotel "hotel" → **hoteli** "hotels"
pivo "beer" → **piva** "beers"

Some have slightly different forms, e.g.

Srbin "Serb" → **Srbi** "Serbs"
dete "child" → **deca** "children"
park "park" → **parkovi** "parks"

While others have different forms, e.g.

čovek "person" → **ljudi** "people"

CASE — Serbian nouns (and adjectives) also add extra endings that depend on where a word appears in a sentence or whether it is used with a preposition. There are specific masculine, feminine and neuter forms, called declensions, plus many variations and irregularities.

The following example of the basic masculine declension for **telefon** ("telephone"), together with its grammatical descriptions, should give you an idea:*

Nominative	**telefon**
Vocative	**telefone**
Accusative	**telefon**
Genitive	**telefona**
Dative	**telefonu**
Instrumental	**telefonom**
Locative	**telefonu**

The first and third cases are used to indicate where the noun is the subject (nominative) or object (accusative) of a verb.

The vocative is used when addressing people — you'll hear this especially in the words **gospodine!** "Sir!", **gospođo!** "Madam!", and **gospođice!** "Miss!"

The remainder of the cases are used where English would employ a preposition, or where a preposition triggers a particular case in the nouns that follows it, e.g.

Genitive	**sok od jabuke** "apple juice" (literally: "juice from apple")
Dative	**bratu** "for [my] brother"
Instrumental	**telefonom** "by telephone"
Locative	**u stanovima** "in the flats"

"OF" — The genitive case also gives you a similar sense as "of" or the English ending -'s, e.g. **flaša vode** "a bottle of water (**voda**)", **datum rođenja** "date of birth (**rođenje**)", **mapa Beograda** "a map of Belgrade (**Beograd**)". Where the English "of" indicates actual possession, for "Dušan's car", you say **Dušanov auto** or **auto od Dušana**.

---

* Note that this is the singular declension only — the plural has a different set of endings.

h = lo*ch*/*h*it   **j** = *y*et   **š** = *sh*ip   **ž** = a*z*ure

—Adjectives

As mentioned in the section on Nouns, adjectives in Serbian generally change according to the gender of the nouns they modify, usually adding **-a** for the feminine form, and **-o/-e** for the neuter. They come before the noun. For examples, see page 20. Some useful adjectives are:

otvoren open	**brz** quick
zatvoren shut	**spor** slow
jeftin cheap	**srećan** happy
skup expensive	**mali** small
vruć hot	**star** old
hladan cold	**mlad** young
veliki big	**dobar** good
dug long	**loš** bad
ogroman huge	**siromašan** poor
majušan tiny	**kratak** short

Some adjectives have varying forms as a result of sound changes or irregularity, e.g. the feminine of **hladan** "cold" is **hladna**, neuter is **hladno**.

Adjectives change gender when speaking about oneself, e.g.

Gladan sam. "I am hungry." *(said by a male)*
Gladna sam. "I am hungry." *(said by a female)*

Žedan sam. "I am thirsty." *(said by a male)*
Žedna sam. "I am thirsty." *(said by a female)*

—Adverbs

Some common adverbs are:

here **ovde**	up **gore**
there **tamo**	down **dole**
well **dobro**	now **sada**

mostly **pretežno**	tomorrow **sutra**
straight on **pravo**	slowly **polako**

—Prepositions

Common prepositions are:

sa; s with	**iz** from; out of
na in; on; at	**od** from; of
kod at	**iznad** above
u in; to	**ispod** below
daleko od far from	**blizu** near to
iza behind	**ispred** in front of
do to	**prema** towards
po around; in	**o** about
k/ka to; towards	**kroz** through

e.g. **kod pozorišta** "at the theater", **blizu parka** "near the park", **sa mesom** "with meat", **novine na engleskom** "newspaper in English", **u Beogradu** "in Belgrade", **iz Amerike** "from America".

The sense of English prepositions is also rendered by grammatical "cases" (see above in the section on nouns).

—Pronouns

Like nouns and adjectives, all pronouns change for gender and case. Basic personal pronouns are as follows:

SINGULAR	PLURAL
I **ja**	we **mi**
you *singular* **ti**	you *plural* **vi**
he **on**	they *masculine* **oni**
she **ona**	they *feminine* **one**
it **ono**	they *neuter* **ona**

Use **vi** also for anyone you don't know well, or who is older or more senior.

As with French or Spanish, possessive pronouns agree in gender with the thing possessed rather than the possessor. Basic forms are:

SINGULAR

my **moj/-a/-e**
your **tvoj/tvoja/tvoje**
his/its **njegov/-a/-o**
her/its **njen/-a/-o**

PLURAL

our **naš/-a/-e**
your **vaš/-a/-e**
their **njohov/-a/-o**

e.g. **moj brat** "my brother"
moja sestra "my sister"
njegova adresa "his address"
njena adresa "her address"

Simple demonstratives in Serbian are:

this **ovaj/ova/ovo**
these **ovi/ove/ova**

that (near you) **taj/ta/to**
those (near you) **ti/te/ta**

that (over there) **onaj/ona/ono**
those (over there) **oni/one/ona**

—Verbs

Verbs are very easy to form, adding a number of prefixes and suffixes to the basic verb form. In fact the underlying structure of Serbian verbs shares similiar concepts with the majority of other European languages, and so its system of regularities and irregularities may soon appear familiar.

piti "to drink"
ja pijem "I drink"
ja sam pio "I drank"
ja sam popio "I have drunk."
ja ću piti "I will drink"

c = hi**ts**   č = **ch**urch   ć = t**y**/**chy**   đ = **dy**   dž = **j**am
24 · Serbian Dictionary & Phrasebook

We saw the personal pronouns above, but these are only used for emphasis. Like French or Spanish, the verb already gives this information:

SINGULAR	PLURAL
I **-am/-em/-im**	we **-amo/-emo/-imo**
you *singular* **-aš/-eš/-iš**	you *plural* **-ate/-ete/-ite**
he/she/it **-a/-e/-i**	they **-aju/-u/-e**

e.g.

govorim I speak	**govorimo** we speak
govoriš you speak	**govorite** you speak
govori he/she/it speaks	**govore** they speak

These are the most commonly used endings (they can take different forms according to the tense used).

As mentioned above, use the second person singular **ti** and **-š** ending to address an individual informally. Use **vi** and the **-te** ending of the second person plural to address two or more people, and also as a formal way of addressing one person or more. When in doubt, always use the formal **vi** form.

The majority of Serbian verbs have two forms, called "perfective" (when the verb's action is completed) and "imperfective" (when the action is ongoing), e.g.

PERFECTIVE	IMPERFECTIVE
popiti	**piti** "to drink"
početi	**počinjati** "to leave"
napisati	**pisati** "to write"
dati	**davati** "to give"
spremiti	**spremati** "to prepare"

e.g. **Popili su kafu.** "They drank their coffee."
Pili su kafu. "They were drinking their coffee."

"Not" is **ne**, e.g. **Razumem.** "I understand." **Ne razumem.** "I don't understand." Note that **ne** also means "no". **Da** means "yes."

"Do not!" is **nemoj/nemojte**, e.g. **nemojte ići!** "don't go!"

QUESTIONS — If you want to create simple questions, **da li** is put at the beginning of sentences or **li** after the first word, e.g.

Razumete srpski.
"You understand Serbian."

Da li razumete srpski? *or* **Razumete li srpski?**
"Do you understand Serbian?"

—Essential verbs

—"To be"
The most useful form of the verb "to be" (**biti**) you will need is the simple series of present endings, which are found in "short" and "long" forms:

SHORT:

SINGULAR	PLURAL
ja sam I am	**mi smo** we are
ti si you are	**vi ste** you are
on/ona/ono je he/she/it is	**oni su** they are

e.g. **Ja sam Srbin.** "I'm a Serb."

LONG:

SINGULAR	PLURAL
jesam I am	**jesmo** we are
jesi you are	**jeste** you are
jeste he/she/it is	**jesu** they are

e.g.   **Vi ste Srbin.** "Are you Serbian?"
      Da, jesam. "Yes, I am."

There is a special negative form, adding **ni-** (a form of not):

SINGULAR	PLURAL
nisam I am not	**nismo** we are not
nisi you are not	**niste** you are not
nije he/she/it is not	**nisu** they are not

e.g. **Nisam gladan.** "I'm not hungry."

—"To have" imati

SINGULAR	PLURAL
imam I have	**imamo** we have
imaš you have	**imate** you have
ima he/she/it has	**imaju** they have

Like "to be" above, **imati** has a short negative form, e.g. **nemam** "I don't have."

Ima also means "there is/there are", e.g. **ima piva** "there is beer". **Nema** means "there is not/there are not", e.g. **nema problema!** no problem! (literally "there are no problems!")

—"To want" hteti

SINGULAR	PLURAL
hoću I want	**hoćemo** we want
hoćeš you want	**hoćete** you want
hoće he/she/it wants	**hoće** they want

Like "to be" above, **hteti** has a short negative form, e.g. **neću** "I don't want."

—"To be able, can" moći

SINGULAR	PLURAL
mogu I can	**možemo** we can
možeš you can	**možete** you can
može he/she/it can	**mogu** they can

—"To like" in its general sense is expressed by **voleti**, but Serbian uses forms that parallel the Spanish *me gusta* or French *il me plaît* (literally "it pleases me"), when expressing like or dislike for something specific.

One common Serbian expression for liking/not

liking is used as in the various forms:

Sviđa mi se... "I like . . ."
Sviđa mi se fudbal. "I like football."
(literally: "Pleases me football.")

Ne sviđa mi se... "I don't like . . ."
Ne sviđa mi se fudbal. "I don't like football."
(literally: "Not pleases me football.")

Sviđa mi se. "I like it."
Ne, ne sviđa mi se. "No, I don't like it." ■

PRONUNCIATION GUIDE

Serbian letter	Serbian example	Approximate English equivalent
a	**avion** "airplane"	**a**pple
b	**banka** "bank"	**b**ox
c	**centar** "center"	hi**ts**
č	**čaj** "tea"	**ch**urch
ć	**ćao!** "hi!"	like **ty** (see Notes)
d	**da** "yes"	**d**og
dž	**pomorandža** "orange"	**j**et
đ	**gospođica** "Miss"	like **dy** (see Notes)
e	**evro** "euro"	p**e**t
f	**fudbal** "soccer"	**f**at
g	**grad** "town"	**g**ot
h	**hvala!** "thank you!"	Scottish lo**ch** or Spanish **j**ota
i	**ime** "name"	h**ea**t
j	**jedan** "one"	**y**es
k	**kafić** "café-bar"	**k**ick
l	**leto** "summer"	**l**et
lj	**ljubav** "love"	like **ly** (see Notes)
m	**more** "sea"	**m**at
n	**novine** "newspaper"	**n**et
nj	**glasanje** "voting"	o**ni**on
o	**oko** "eye"	c**o**t, in South British English
p	**policija** "police"	**p**et
r	**restoran** "restaurant"	**r**at, but "rolled' as in Scottish English
s	**sneg** "snow"	**s**it
š	**škola** "school"	**sh**ut
t	**telefon** "telephone"	**t**en
u	**ulica** "street"	sh**oo**t
v	**voda** "water"	**v**an
z	**zemlja** "country"	**z**ebra
ž	**žurka** "party"	a**z**ure or plea**s**ure

h = lo**ch**/**h**it   j = **y**et   š = **sh**ip   ž = a**z**ure

Nothing beats listening to a native speaker, but the following notes should help give you some idea of how to pronounce the following letters. Remember that Serbian is one of the few European languages which is spelled the way it is pronounced and pronounced the way it is written. (Note, however, that vowels can be short or long. This rarely affects meaning, however, and is not indicated in the Serbian alphabet.)

—Vowels

Apart from the vowels mentioned above, note these combinations with **j**:

aj is pronounced as the "y" in English "sk*y*", e.g. **kraj** "area" (= *"kry"*).

ej is pronounced as the "ey" in English "h*ey*", e.g. **imejl** "email" (= *"imeyl"*).

oj is pronounced as the "oy" in English "b*oy*", e.g. **broj** "number" (= *"broy"*).

—Consonants

ć is pronounced similar to *ty*, e.g. **ćao!** "hi!" is pronounced as *"tyao!"* The English equivalent is the pronunciation of "tune" by most British English speakers as *"tyune"*. Note that in both Serbian and English this can also sound closer to a form of *chy* (i.e Serbian **ćao!** = *"chyao!"* and English "tune" = *"chyune"*).

đ is pronounced similar to *dy*, e.g. **gospođica** "Miss" is pronounced as *"gospodyitsa"* (remember that **c** = *ts*). The English equivalent is the pronunciation of "due" by most British English speakers, as *"dyue"*. Note that in both Serbian and English this can also sound closer to a form of *jy* (i.e Serbian **gospođica** = *"gospojyitsa"* and English "due" = *"jyune"*).

h is the rasping "ch" in Scottish "lo*ch*", German "a*ch*", or the Spanish/Castillian "jota" in "*j*amás". This sound is generally much softer and can sometimes appear similar to a "heavy" English "h".

─Sound changes

l A feature of the Serbian sound system is that the letter "L" is frequently dropped or appears, e.g. **beo** "white" is the adjective's masculine form, but it becomes **bela** in the feminine and **belo** in the neuter. Similarly, the Serbian capital "Belgrade" is **Beograd**.

r In words like **Srbija** ("Serbia"), **trg** ("town square") and **prvi** ("first"), the vowel (like the English neutral "e" in "open") that is pronounced in front of the **r** is always predictible and therefore not written, e.g. **Srbija** is pronounced "S[e]rbiya" and **trg** as "t[e]rg", and **prvi** as "p[e]rvi" (the stronger you roll the **r**, the less you hear the "uh" of the "e"!)

─Spelling & usage notes

1) Capital letter forms of Serbian letters not found in English are as follows:

č	Č
ć	Ć
đ	Đ
dž	Dž
š	Š
ž	Ž

2) **đ** is also frequently written as **dj**.

3) Note that the combinations **dž**, **lj** and **nj** (plus **dj** if used) are considered distinct letters and so are listed separately in the dictionary section.

4) Abbreviations used are *m* (male/man), *f* (female/woman), and *pl* (plural/people).

5) Nationalities are generally given in their male and female forms, e.g. **Amerikanac/Amerikanka** means "American *male person*/American *female person*".

6) Unless noted otherwise, adjectives are given in their masculine form only. The feminine and neuter forms are predictable in most cases, e.g. **nov** "new" gives the feminine **nova** and neuter **novo**. ∎

The Serbian alphabet (Cyrillic)

Serban letter	Roman equivalent
Аа	a
Бб	b
Вв	v
Гг	g
Дд	d
Ђђ	dj (đ)
Ее	e
Жж	ž
Зз	z
Ии	i
Јј	j
Кк	k
Лл	l
Љљ	lj
Мм	m
Нн	n
Њњ	nj
Оо	o
Пп	p
Рр	r
Сс	s
Тт	t
Ћћ	ć
Уу	u
Фф	f
Хх	h
Цц	c
Чч	č
Џџ	dž
Шш	š

č = church   ć = ty/chy   đ = dy   dž = jam

SERBIAN
Dictionary

SERBIAN–ENGLISH
SRPSKI–ENGLESKI

A

a but
adapter *electric* adapter
administracija administration
adresa address
adresar directory
advokat lawyer
aerodrom airport; airbase
agrikultura agriculture
agronom agronomist
akademija academy
aker acre
ako if; **ako je moguće** if
  possible; **ako ne** unless
alat tools
alergičan allergic
ali but; however
alkohol alcohol; **alkoholno piće**
  liquor
ambasada embassy
ambasador ambassador
ambulanta ambulance
američki American *thing*
Amerika America
Amerikanac/Amerikanka American *person*
amputirati to amputate
anelgetik painkiller
anemija anemia
anestezija; anestetik anesthetic
antibiotik antibiotic
antifriz anti-freeze
antiseptik antiseptic
apetit appetite
apoteka pharmacy
april April
Arapin Arab
arapski Arabic *language/ thing*

arhitekta architect
armija army
arsenal arsenal
arterija artery
artiljerija artillery
aspirin aspirin
astma asthma
ateista atheist
atentat assassination
atletika athletics
atomski atomic
auspuh exhaust *of car*
Australija Australia
Australijanac/Australijanka
  Australian *person*
australijski Australian *thing*
auto car
autobus bus; **autobusom** by
  bus
autobuska stanica bus stop; bus
  station
automobil car
autoput highway; motorway
autor author
averzija aversion
avijacija aviation
avion airplane; **Avion kasni.** The
  plane is delayed.
avionsko pismo air mail letter
Azija Asia

B

baba grandmother
babica midwife
bacili germs
baciti to throw
badem almond
bajat stale *bread*

bajka story; tale
bajonet bayonet
bakar copper
bakterija bacteria; **bakterije** germs
balkon balcony
banana banana
banka bank
bankar banker
bar bar
bašta garden; yard
baština: narodna baština folklore
baštovan gardener
baterija *electric* battery
baterijska lampa torch; flashlight
bazen swimming pool
beba baby
beg flight; escape
bela rotkva turnip
beli luk garlic
beličast whitish
belo white
benzin petrol; gasoline; **Nestalo mi benzina.** I have run out of petrol.
beo white
berberin barber
beskućnik homeless person
besnilo rabies
besplatan free of charge
bešika bladder
bez without; -less; **bez oca** fatherless; **bez posla** without work; **bez soli** saltless; **bez šećera** no sugar
bezbedan safe
bezbednost safety
bezukusan tasteless
bezuspešan unsuccessful
bežati to flee; to escape
beživotan lifeless
biber pepper *spice*
Biblija Bible
biblioteka library
bicikl bicycle

biftek steak
bik bull
biletarnica ticket office *in theater/cinema*
bilo da whether
bilo gde anywhere
bilo ko anyone
bilo šta whatever
biljka plant *botanical*
bioskop cinema
birati to dial; **Treba li da biram ovaj broj?** Should I dial this number?
birokratija bureaucracy
biser pearl
bistar intelligent
biti to be; **biti bolestan** to be ill; **biti zabrinut** to be worried; *and see page 26*
bitka fight; battle
biznismen businessman
blagajnik cashier
blato mud
bled pale
blesak flash
blic flash
blindirana kola armored car
blizanci twins
blizu near
blokiran blocked; **Ve-ce je blokiran.** The toilet is blocked.
bljesak lightning
bljutav stale *taste*
bobica berry
boca flask; **boca za vodu** water bottle
bodljikava žica barbed wire
bog God
bogat rich
boja color; paint
bojati se to fear
bojiti to paint
bokal jug
boks boxing *sport*
bol grief
bol pain; **bol u leđima**

c = hi*ts*   č = *ch*urch   ć = *ty/chy*   d = d*y*   dž = *j*am

backache; **bol u stomaku** stomachache

bolan sore

bolest illness; disease

bolestan ill; **Bolestan sam.** I am ill.

bolnica hospital

bolji better; **Bolje se osećam.** I feel better.

bomba bomb

bombardovanje bombardment

bonbona candy

bonton etiquette

borac fighter

boranija green beans

borba struggle

bording karta boarding pass

boriti se to fight

bos barefoot

braća brothers

brada chin; beard

brak marriage

brak: razvod braka divorce

brana dam

branik bumper *of car*

braon brown

brašno flour

brat brother; *male* cousin; **stariji brat** elder brother

bratanac nephew *brother's son*

bratanica niece *brother's daughter*

brati to reap

brava door lock

brazda furrow

brdo hill

breskva peach; **breskve** peaches

briga trouble; problem

brijač razor

brijanje shave; shaving; **pena za brijanje** shaving cream

brinuti to be worried; to tend *to the sick*

brisanje: gumica za brisanje eraser

Britanac *male* Briton

Britanija Britain

Britanka *female* Briton

britanski British *thing*

brk; brkovi mustache

brod ship; **brod za prevoz nafte** oil tanker

broj number; **broj pasoša** passport number; **broj perona** platform number

brojati count

brošura brochure; pamphlet

brus-halter brassiere

brz fast; quick

brzak mountain stream

brzina speed; gear

brzo quickly

bubanj drum

buba-švaba cockroach

bubna opna ear drum

bubreg kidney; **bubrezi** kidneys

budala fool

budan awake

Budi(te) strpljivi! Be patient!

budilnik alarm clock

budućnost future

budžet budget

buka noise

buna riot

bundeva pumpkin

buntovnik rebel

bura gale

bure *storage* barrel

bušiti to drill

bušotina oil well

butina thigh

buva flea

C

carina border customs; *customs* duty

ce de C.D. (compact disc)

cediti to squeeze

cena price

ceniti to value

centar center

centar grada city center; town center

centrala telephone operator

ceo whole; **ceo svet** all the world

cepati to tear

cev pipe; barrel *of gun*

cevanica tibia

cigareta cigarette; **cigarete** cigarettes

cigla brick

cilj aim; destination

cipela shoe; **cipele** shoes

crevo hose

creva intestine(s)

crkva church

crn black

crni luk onion

crpiti to pump; **crpiti vodu** to pump water

crta line

crtati to draw *an image*

crtež drawing; picture

crven red

Crveni krst Red Cross

crvi worms

curiti to leak

cvećar florist

cvekla beetroot; beet

cvet flower

cvrčak cricket *insect*

Č

čačkalica toothpick

čaj tea

čajdžinica tea house

čajnik kettle; teapot

čak even

čak iako even if

čanak bowl

čarape socks

čaršav sheet *of cloth*

čas lesson; period; class

časopis magazine

čast honor

čaša *drinking* glass; **čaša vode** glass of water

ček bank check

čekaj(te)! wait a moment!

čekanje waiting

čekati to wait; to wait for

čekić hammer

čekiranje check-in

čeličan *adjective* steel

čelik steel

čelo forehead

čeljad livestock

čep *bath* plug; cork

česma tap

često often

češalj comb

četiri four

četka brush; hairbrush; **četkica za zube** toothbrush

četrdeset forty

četrnaest fourteen

četvrt quarter; **četvrt sata** quarter of an hour

četvrtak Thursday

četvrtgodišnje quarterly

četvrti fourth

četvrtina quarter

činjenica fact

čir ulcer; **čir na želudcu** stomach ulcer

čist *adjective* clean; **čista posteljina** clean sheets

čistiti to clean; to clear

čitanje reading

čitaonica library

čitati to read

čizme boots

član member

članak ankle; article

čoban shepherd

čokolada chocolate

čovečiji *adjective* human

čovek man

čudan strange

čudo miracle

čukununuk great-great-grandson

čukununuka great-great-granddaughter

čuti to hear

c = hi**ts**   č = **ch**urch   ć = t**y**/**chy**   d = d**y**   dž = **j**am

čuvar guard; **noćni čuvar** night-guard; nightwatchman
čvrst tight

Ć

ćebe blanket
ćevapi kebab
ćilim *woven* carpet
ćumur charcoal(s)
ćup pot
ćurka turkey
ćutati to be quiet
ćutljiv silent

D

da yes; *conjunction* that; **da li** whether
dakle so; therefore
daleko far
dalje *preposition* beyond
Danac *male* Dane
danas today; **danas posle podne** this afternoon
Dankinja *female* Dane
danski Danish
daska plank
daščica *medical* splint
dati to give; **dati go** to score a goal; **daj(te) mi** give me...
datum date *time;* **datum dolaska** date of arrival; **datum odlaska** date of departure; **datum rođenja** date of birth; **Koji je danas datum?** What's the date today?
davno long ago
debata dicussion
debeo fat; wide
deblo trunk *of tree*
deca children
decembar December
decenija decade
dečak boy; child
dečiji lekar pediatrician

deda grandfather
deklaracija declaration
deliti to share
deljenje division
demokratija democracy
demonstracije *political* demonstration
demonstratori *political* demonstrators
deo part
deset ten
desna ruka right hand
desni gum; gums
desnica right-wing
desno right *side;* **s desne strane** to the right
dete child; infant
detelina clover
deterdžent detergent
detonacija detonation
detonirati to detonate
devedeset ninety
dever brother-in-law *husband's brother*
devet nine
devetnaest nineteen
devojčica child; girl
devojka girlfriend; girl; teenager
devojke girls
dezert dessert
dezodorans deodorant
digitron calculator
dijabetes diabetes
dijabetičar diabetic
dijagnoza *medical* diagnosis
dijalekt dialect
dijaspora diaspora
dijeta diet
dim smoke
dimnjak chimney
dinamo dynamo
dinja melon
diplomata diplomat
diplomatske veze diplomatic ties
direkcija director's office
direktan *adjective* direct

h = lo*ch*/hit   j = yet   š = *sh*ip   ž = a*z*ure

direktor director; **direktor škole** headmaster/principal
direktorat director's office
disati breathe
diskusija dicussion
diskutovati to discuss
divlja životinja wild animal
dizalica crane *machine*
dizel gorivo diesel
dizenterija dysentery
dlan palm *of hand*
dnevne novine daily newspaper
dnevno daily
dno bottom *level*
do until
doba period; season
dobar *adjective* good; well
dobitak gain
dobiti to get
dobro good; well; **dobro i zlo** good and evil
dobrodošli! welcome!
dobrodušan *adjective* kind
dobrotvorna organizacija charity *organization*
doći to come
dodatan extra
dodati to add
dogoditi se to happen
dogovori *plural* arrangements
dojka breast
dok while
dokaz proof
dokazati to prove
doktor doctor
dokument document
dolar dollar
dole under; down
dolina valley
domaća životinja domestic animal
domaći zadatak homework
domaćin host
domar janitor
doneti to bring
donji novo bottom *level*
donji veš underwear

dopisnica postcard
doručak breakfast
doseći to reach; to arrive at
doseljenje immigration
dosta enough
doviđenja! good-bye!
dovoljan sufficient
dovoljno enough
dozvoliti to allow
dozvoljen permitted
drag(i) dear; loved
dragocenosti jewelry
drama *theater* drama; play
drevni ancient
droga drug; narcotic
drug companion
drugačiji different
drugi; drugačiji other; another
društven social; **društvena zajednica** community
društvo society
drva za potpalu firewood
drveće trees
drvena olovka pencil
drvo tree; wood
držati to hold; to keep
država *federal* state; **nezavisna država** independent state
državljanin citizen
državljanstvo citizenship
dubina depth
dubok deep
dud mulberry
dug debt
duga rainbow
dugačak long; big
dugme button
duh mind
duša soul
dušek mattress
dušnik trachea
duvan tobacco
duvati to blow
dužina length
dužnost duty; commission
dva two
dvadeset twenty

c = hi*ts*   č = *ch*urch   ć = t*y/chy*   d = *dy*   dž = *j*am

dvanaest twelve
dvaput twice
dve nedelje fortnight
dvogled binoculars
dvogodišnji biannual
dvopek toast *bread*
dvorište yard *courtyard*

DŽ

džak sack
džamija mosque
džem jam
džemper sweater; jumper
džep pocket
džez jazz

Đ

đak school pupil
đavo devil
đon sole
đubre rubbish; trash
đubrivo fertilizer; manure
đumbir ginger

E

egzaktan exact
ekcem eczema
ekipa team
ekonomija economics; economy *of country*
ekonomista economist
ekser *metal* nail
eksplodirati to explode
eksplozija explosion
eksploziv(i) explosives
ekspres express; fast
ekstradicija extradition
ekvivalentan equivalent
električna pošta e-mail
električni udar electric shock
emisija radio program
Engleska England
engleski English *language/thing*; **engleske novine** newspaper in English
Engleskinja Englishwoman
Englez Englishman
enterijer *noun* interior
epidemija epidemic
epilepsija epilepsy
esej essay
etiketa etiquette
evakuisati to evacuate
evro euro *currency*
Evropa Europe
Evropska Zajednica; Evropska Unija European Union
evropski European

F

fabrika factory
fajl *computer* file
faks fax
fakultet college; faculty; *informal* degree
falsifikat counterfeit
falsifikovan: Ovaj novac je falsifikovan. This money is counterfeit.
farbati to paint
farma farm
fascikla *paper* file
fazan pheasant
februar February
feder *metal* spring
federacija federation
fen hairdryer
fenjer lantern
feribot ferry
festival festival; **filmski festival** film festival; **muzički festival** music festival
fijoka drawer
film *movie/camera* film
filmski festival film festival
filmski reditelj filmmaker
filter filter
fin(o) fine
finale *noun* final

h = lo*ch*/*h*it   j = *y*et   š = *sh*ip   ž = a*z*ure

finansije finance; financial affairs

firma company; firm

fizički physical; **fizička aktivnost** exercise; activity

fizika physics

fizioterapija physiotherapy

flaster Band-Aid; plaster

flaša bottle; **flaša vode** bottle of water

flomaster felt-tip pen

folklor folklore

folklorna igra folk dancing

folklorna muzika folk music

fondacija foundation; organisation

formular *official* form; **popuniti formular** to fill in a form

fotoaparat camera

fotograf photographer

fotografija photo; photography

fotokopija photocopy

fotokopir mašina photocopier

fotokopirati to photocopy

fotokopirnica photocopier

francuski French *language/thing*

Francuskinja Frenchwoman

Francuz Frenchman

frizer hairdresser

frižider refrigerator

front *military* front

fudbal football

fudbalska utakmica football match

funta pound *weight/sterling*

G

ga him

gajiti to grow crops

gajtan cable

galama noise

galon gallon

gangrena gangrene

garaža garage

garnizon garrison

gazda landlord

gazela gazelle

gde where; **gde je?** where is?; **gde su?** where are?

general *noun* general

generalan *adjective* general

genitalije genitals

genocid genocide

geografija geography

geolog geologist

gepek trunk/boot *of car*

gerila guerrilla

ginekolog gynecologist

gips plaster; plaster cast

glad hunger; famine

gladak smooth

gladan hungry; **Gladan sam.** I'm hungry.

glagol verb

glas voice; vote

glasač voter

glasan loud

glasanje voting

glasati to vote

glasno loudly

glava head; boss

glavni *adjective* main; **glavni grad** capital city; **glavni trg** main square

glavobolja headache

glečer glacier

gledati to look; to watch

gliste *stomach* worms

gluposti trash

gluv deaf

go naked; goal; **Ko je dao go?** Who scored? *in football*

godina year

godišnji annual; **godišnje doba** season

godišnjica anniversary

gol *football* goal

golub pigeon

golubica dove

goniti to chase

gorak bitter

gore above; up; worse; **Osećam se gore.** I feel worse.

goreti to burn

c = hi*ts*   č = *ch*urch   ć = *ty/chy*   d = *dy*   dž = *j*am

gorivo fuel
gospodin gentleman; Mr.
gospođa Mrs.
gospođica Miss
gost guest
gostionica hostel; guesthouse; restaurant
gostoljubiv hospitable
gostoprimljiv hospitable
govedina beef
govoriti to speak; **Govorite li engleski?** Do you speak English?; **Govorim engleski.** I speak English.
govornica public phone
govornik speaker; speaker *of parliament*
gozba feast
grad city; town; hail
graditi build
gradski trg town square
građanin/građanski civilian
građanska prava civil rights
građanski rat civil war
građevina structure
grafitna olovka pencil
gram gram
gramatika grammar
gramofonska ploča *noun* record
grana branch
granata grenade; shell
granica border; limit
granice limits
graničar border guard
grašak peas
Grčka Greece
grčki Greek *language/thing*
greda beam *girder*
grejpfrut grapefruit
greška mistake
grickalice snacks
grip flu
Grk/Grkinja Greek *person*
grlo throat
grob *noun* grave
groblje cemetery

grobnica tomb
grom thunder
groznica fever
grožđe grapes
grub rough; coarse
grud chest; breast
grudni koš rib cage
grupa group
gudura ravine
guja viper
guma gum; tire/tyre; **rezervna guma** spare tire; **izduvana guma** flat tire; **Ispustila mi je guma.** I have a flat tire.
gumene čizme rubber boots
gumica za brisanje rubber; eraser
gurati to push
gusenica caterpillar
guska goose
gušiti se to choke; **On/ona se guši!** He/She is choking!
gušter lizard
gušterača pancreas
gutati to swallow
gužva traffic jam
gvožđarija hardware store

H

hajdemo! Let's go!
haljina dress
hangar hangar
hanzaplast Band-Aid; plaster
hapšenje arrest
hartija paper; sheet *of paper*
hašiš hashish
hauba hood/bonnet *of car*
helikopter helicopter
hemija chemistry
hemijska olovka biro; pen
hemijski chemical
hepatitis hepatitis
heroj hero
higijena hygiene
hiljadu thousand

h = lo*ch*/*hit*   j = yet   š = *sh*ip   ž = azure

hirurg surgeon
hirurgija surgery
hirurški surgical; **hirurška operacija** surgery; operation
hitno urgently
hlad shade *from sun*
hladan cool; cold; **hladna voda** cold water; **Hladno je.** It is cold.; **Hladno mi je.** I am cold.
hladnoća *noun* cold
hleb bread; loaf
hodnik corridor
hodočasnik pilgrim
hodočašće pilgrimage; **ići u hodočašće** to go on pilgrimage
holandski Dutch *language/ thing*
Holanđanin Dutchman
Holanđanka Dutchwoman
hotel hotel
hrabar brave
hrabrost courage
hram temple
hrana food
hraniti to feed
hrišćanin/hrišćanka Christian *person*
hrišćanstvo Christianity
hrkati to snore
Hrvat/Hrvatica Croatian *person*
Hrvatska Croatia
hrvatski Croatian *thing*
humanitaran humanitarian
humanitarna pomoć humanitarian aid
humor humor
hvala! thank you!

I

i and
iako although; **čak iako** even if
ići to go; **ići na spavanje** to go to bed; **ići u rikverc** to reverse *a car*; **ići unazad** to go backwards

ideal *political* cause
ideja idea
identifikacija I.D.; pass
idi! go!
igla needle; pin
igra dance; game
igralište ring; *football* pitch
igranje dancing
igrati (se) to play; to perform
ilegalan illegal
ili or; **ili...ili** either ... or
ima... there is/are ...
imati to have
ime name; **Kako je vaše ime?** What is your name?; **Moje ime je Fred.** My name is Fred.
imejl e-mail; **imejl adresa** e-mail address
imenica noun
imigracija immigration
imigrant immigrant
Indija India
indijski Indian *thing*
industrija industry
infekcija infection
informacija information; **(služba za) informacije** information office
insekt bug; insect; **insekti** insects
insekticid insecticide
institut institute
instrukcija instruction; teaching
inteligencija intelligence
inteligentan intelligent
interes *financial* interest
interesantan interesting
interesovanje interest
interesovati se to be interested
internet internet
interval interval
intervju interview
invalid disabled person
invalidska kolica wheelchair
invazija invasion
inženjer engineer
Irac Irishman
Iran Iran

Iranac/Iranka Iranian *person*
iranski Iranian *thing*
Irkinja Irishwoman
Irska Ireland
irski Irish *language/thing*
iscrpljenost exhaustion
isključiti to switch off
islam Islam
islamski Islamic
ispit test; exam
ispitivanje test; inquiry
ispitivati to test
isplata payment
ispod below; under; **ispod stola** under the table
isporučiti to hand over
ispravan right; correct
isprave documents
ispraviti to correct
ispred in front of
ispunjen full
istaživati to investigate
isti same
istina truth
istinit true
istočan east(ern)
istok *noun* east
istoričar historian
istorija history
istraga inquiry; investigation
istraživanje research; study
istraživati to research
Italija Italy
Italijan/Italijanka Italian *person*
italijanski Italian *language/ thing*
iz from
iza behind
izabrati to choose; to elect
izaći to go out
izbaciti to throw out
izbeći to escape
izbeglica refugee; **izbeglice** refugees
izbeglički centar refugee camp
izbor(i) election(s)
izdavač publisher

izduvana guma flat tire
izgledati to seem
izgovor pronunciation; excuse
izgovoriti to pronounce
izgubiti to lose; **Izgubio sam ključ.** I have lost my key.; **Izgubio sam se.** I am lost.
izlaz exit; **izlaz u nuždi** emergency exit
izlazak sunca sunrise
izlečiti to heal
izlet picnic
izložba show; fair
izmaglica mist
između between
iznad above; upon
iznajmiti to hire; to rent
iznenada suddenly
iznenađen surprised
iznenađujuć surprising
izneti to take out
iznos amount
izopačen corrupt
Izrael Israel
Izraelac/Izraelka Israeli *person*
izraelski Israeli *thing*
izraz; izražavanje expression
izručivanje zločinaca extradition
izuzev apart from; except
izvan out
izvesti to perform; to export
izvestiti to report
izveštač reporter
izveštaj report *news*
izvidnica patrol
izvijač spanner; wrench
izvinite! excuse me!; sorry!
izvod *noun* extract; **izvod iz matične knjige rođenih** birth certificate
izvođenje performance
izvor source; spring; well *of water*
izvoz exports
izvoziti to export
izvršitelj administrator
izvršiti to carry out; **izvršiti**

h = loc**h**/**h**it   j = **y**et   š = **sh**ip   ž = a**z**ure

ubistvo to murder; **izvršiti invaziju** to invade
izvršni administrative; **izvršni rukovodilac** executive
izvući to pull out

J

ja I
jabuka apple
jagnje lamb
jagnjetina lamb *meat*
jagoda strawberry
jahanje horseback riding
jahati to ride *a horse*
jaje egg; **kuvano jaje** boiled egg
jak strong; severe; **jaka vrućina** severe heat
jakna jacket
januar January
Japan Japan
Japanac/Japanka Japanese *person*
japanski Japanese *language/thing*
jarac goat
jarda yard *distance*
jare kid *goat*
jarebica partridge
jaretina goat meat
jasan *adjective* clear
jastučić cushion
jastuk pillow
javiti to report
javni telefon pay-phone
je is; her
ječam barley
jedan one; single
jedanaest eleven
jedini only; alone
jedinica unit *military*
jedino *adverb* only
jedinstven unique
jednak equal
jednak equivalent
jednokrevetna soba single room
jednom once

jednosmerna ulica one-way street
jednostavan simple
jeftin cheap
jeftiniji cheaper
jelen deer
jelovnik menu
jesen fall; autumn
jesti to eat
jestiv edible
jetra liver
jetrva sister-in-law *husband's brother's wife*
Jevrejin/Jevrejka Jew
jevrejski Jewish
jezero lake
jezik language; tongue
jež hedgehog
jogurt yogurt
joj her
jorgan duvet
još still; yet; **još jednu flašu** another bottle
juče yesterday
jučerašnji yesterday's
judaizam Judaism
jug *noun* south
juli July
juni June
junior junior
jutro morning; acre
jutros this morning
juvelir jeweler
južni south(ern)

K

kabinet *political* cabinet
kabl cable
kad; kada when
kafa coffee; **bela kafa** coffee with milk
kaiš belt
kajsija apricot
kako? how?
kalendar calendar
kamata *financial* interest

---

c = hi*ts*   č = *ch*urch   ć = *ty/chy*   đ = *dy*   dž = *j*am

kamen stone
kamenčić pebble
kamion truck; lorry
kamp camp
kampanja campaign
kamuflaža camouflage
Kanada Canada
Kanađanin/Kanađanka Canadian *person*
kanal canal; **televizijski kanal** T.V. channel
kanalizacija drain
kancelarija office
kanta za ulje oilcan
kantina feeding station
kao *preposition* like
kapija gate
kapital *financial* capital
kaput coat; overcoat
karfiol cauliflower
karmin lipstick
karta ticket; fare; **karta u jednom pravcu** one-way ticket
kaseta tape; cassette
kasetofon tape recorder
kasir cashier
kasnije afterwards
kasniti to be late; **Kasnim.** I am late.; **Avion kasni.** The plane is delayed.
kasno late
kašalj cough
kašičica teaspoon
kašika spoon
kašljati to cough
katanac padlock
katetar catheter
kavez cage
kazna fine *of money*
kazniti to punish
kažiprst index finger
kćer; kćerka daughter; **kćeri; kćerke** daughters
keramika ceramics
kesa carrier bag
kičma spine

kičmeni stub spinal column
kidnaper kidnapper
kidnapovanje kidnapping
kidnapovati to kidnap
kijanje sneeze
kijati to sneeze
kilogram kilogram
kilometar kilometer
Kina China
kineski Chinese *thing*
Kinez/Kineskinja Chinese *person*
kiosk kiosk
kiosk newsstand
kip statue
kirija to rent *for oneself*
kiselo mleko yogurt
kiseo sour
kiseonik oxygen
kiša rain
kišobran umbrella
klan clan
klati to slaughter
klavir piano
klečati to kneel
klica sprout
klima climate
klima uređaj air conditioner
klinika clinic
klizav slippery
klopka trap; ambush
klub club; **noćni klub** nightclub
klupa bench
ključ key
knjiga book
knjižara bookshop; stationer's shop
književnost literature; fiction
ko who; which
kobac sparrowhawk
kobasica sausage
kobila mare
kockati se to gamble
kočiti to brake
kočnica brake
kod at

h = lo*ch*/*h*it   j = *y*et   š = *sh*ip   ž = a*z*ure

kofa bucket
kofer suitcase
koje vrste? what kind?
koji which
kokoška hen
kola car; carriage
kolač cake
koledž college
kolega colleague
koleno knee
kolera cholera
kolevka cradle
količina amount
koliko? how; how many?; how much?; **Koliko košta?** how much is it?
kolosek track
komad piece; **komad mesa** steak
komadić bit
komanda command
komarac mosquito
komentar commentary
komin cumin
komisija committee; commission
kompanija company; firm
kompas compass
kompenzacija compensation
kompjuter computer
kompjuterski program computer program
kompjuterski virus computer virus
komplet set
komšija neighbor
komunikacije communications
konac thread
koncert concert
koncertna dvorana concert hall
kondom condom
konferencija conference; **sala za konferencije** conference room
konobar waiter
konobarica waitress
konopac rope; **konopac za**

vučenje tow rope
konstitucija constitution
konsultant consultant
konsultovati se to consult
kontakt contact
kontaktirati to contact; **Želim da kontaktiram svoju ambasadu.** I want to contact my embassy.
kontracepcija birth control
kontrolisati to control
konzerva tin; can
konzulat, consulate
konj horse; **konji** horses
konjske trke horse racing
kopati to dig; **kopati bunar** to drill a well
kopče *surgical* stitches
kopija copy
kopirati to copy
korak pace
koren root
korisnost usefulness
korist advantage
korist interest
korist use; **korist: u korist...** for the sake of
koristan useful
koristiti to use
korpa basket
korumpiran corrupt
korupcija corruption
kosa hair
kost bone
koš basket
košarka basketball
koštana srž marrow *of bone*
koštati to cost
košulja shirt
kovač blacksmith
koverat envelope
kozje mleko goat's milk
koža skin; leather
kradljivac thief
krađa theft
kragna collar
kraj end

c = hi*ts*   č = *ch*urch   ć = t*y*/*chy*   d = *dy*   dž = *j*am

kralj king
kraljevski royal
kraljica queen
krasta boil
krastavac cucumber
krasti to steal
kratak short
krava cow
kravata tie; necktie
kravlje mleko cow's milk
kreda chalk
kredit credit; **kredit za kuću** mortgage
kreditna kartica credit card
krema cream; ointment; **krema za sunčanje** sunblock
krevet bed
krevetac cot
kriminal crime
kriminalac criminal
kritika review *article*
kriza crisis
krojač tailor; dressmaker
krompir potato
krov roof
kroz through; by means of
krtica mole *animal*
krug ring; circle
krupan large
kruška pear
krv blood; **vađenje krvi** blood test
krvariti to bleed
krvna grupa blood group
krvna osveta feud
krvni pritisak blood pressure
kucati na mašini to type
kucati to knock
kuća house
kućni nadzornik janitor
kuhinja kitchen
kuk hip
kuka hook
kukuruz corn; maize
kula tower
kultivisati to cultivate

kultura culture
kupaći kostim swimsuit
kupac buyer
kupati (se) to bathe
kupatilo bathroom
kupiti to buy
kupovanje buying
kupovina shopping
kupus cabbage
Kuran Quran
kusur change *of money*
kutija box; chest
kutija packet; carton
kutlača ladle
kuvan cooked; **kuvano jaje** boiled egg
kuvar cook
kuvati to cook; **kuvati na pari** to steam *food*
kvačilo clutch *of car*
kvadrat square

L

laboratorija laboratory
lagati to lie; to tell a lie
lajati to bark
lak light *not heavy*
lakat elbow
lako easy
lakoća ease
laku noć! good night!
lampa lamp
lanac chain
laptop laptop *computer*
lasica ferret
lasta swallow *bird*
lav lion
lavabo basin
lavina avalanche
lavor washbowl
lažan false
leblebije chickpeas
lečenje to cure
leći to lie down
led ice
leden icy

leđa

leđa *noun* back
legalan legal
legenda legend
lek medicine; **lek protiv bolova** painkiller; **lek za umirenje** tranquilizer
lekcija lesson
lenj lazy
lenjir ruler *instrument*
lenjost laziness
leopard leopard
lep nice; beautiful
lepak glue
lepeza fan
lepota beauty
leptir butterfly
let *plane* flight; **Želim da potvrdim let.** I want to confirm my flight.
leteti to fly
leto summer
levica left-wing
levo left *side*
levoruk left-handed
ležati to lie; to lie down
lice face; front; person
lična karta I.D.
lift lift; elevator
lik image
limenka tin; can
limun lemon; lime
lingvist linguist
lingvistika linguistics
linija line
lisica fox
list calf *leg*; leaf
lista list
lišaj eczema
litar liter
literatura literature
livada meadow
lizati to lick
lobanja skull
lokacija location
lokal local
lokomotiva locomotive
lonac cooking pot

lončarstvo pottery
lonče kettle
lopata shovel
lopata spade
lopatica shoulder blade
lopov thief; **lopovi** thieves
lopta ball
loš bad
loše badly
loše varenje indigestion
loto lottery
lov hunting
loza vine
lubenica watermelon
luckast silly
lud insane
luka *naval* port
lula *smoking* pipe
lutka doll

LJ

ljubav *noun* love
ljubavna pesma love song
ljubazan kind; polite
ljubičast purple
ljudi people; men
ljudska prava human rights
ljudski *adjective* human; **ljudsko biće** human; human being
ljut angry; spicy; hot

M

mač machete
mačka cat
maćeha stepmother
magarac donkey
magazin magazine
magla fog; mist
maglovito foggy
magnetni magnetic
maj May
majčino mleko human milk
majka mother; **majke** mothers
majmun monkey
makaroni pasta
makaze scissors

c = hi*ts*   č = *ch*urch   ć = t*y*/*chy*   d = d*y*   dž = *j*am

malarija malaria
mali little; small
malić little finger
malo po malo little by little
malopre a moment ago
manastir monastery
manjak lack
manje little; less
manjina minority
mapa map; **mapa grada** city map; **mapa Beograda** map of Belgrade
marama *woman's* headscarf
maramica handkerchief
mari: Ne mari! It doesn't matter!
markica *postal* stamp
mart March
mas mediji mass media
maskara mascara
maslac butter
mast *noun* fat; **mast za rane** ointment
mastilo ink
mašina machine; **mašina za šivenje** sewing machine
mašinka machine gun
mašna tie; necktie
mašta imagination
matematika mathematics; maths
materica womb
materija matter; subject
materijal cloth; material
mazga mule
me me
mećava blizzard
med honey
medicina medicine
medicinska sestra nurse
medicinski *adjective* medical
mediji media
medikament medication
medved bear
među among
međunarodna centrala international operator
međunarodni international

međunarodni let international flight
međunarodni pozivni broj international dialing code
međutim however
mehaničar mechanic
mek soft
memorija memory
menadžer manager
mene; meni me
menstruacija *menstrual* period
menta mint
mera meter *measure*
merdevine ladder
merilo meter *measure*
meriti to measure
mesar butcher
mesec month
Mesec moon
mesečno monthly
mesiti hleb to make bread
meso meat
mesto place; *political* seat; **mesto rođenja** place of birth
mešati to stir
metak bullet
metal *noun* metal
metalan *adjective* metal
metalna kutija canister
metalni novac coins
metar meter
metro metro
meze snack
mi we; us; ourselves
milenijum millennium
milicija police
milion million
milosrđe charity *general notion*
milja mile
mina mine *explosive*
minaret minaret
mineral *noun* mineral
mineralna voda mineral water
ministarstvo ministry
ministarstvo finansija treasury *ministry*
minister minister

minski mine *explosive*; **minsko polje** minefield
minut *noun* minute
mir peace
miran *adjective* quiet
miraz dowry
miris smell; perfume
mirno quietly
mirovne snage/trupe peace-keeping troops
mirovni pregovori peace talks
misao thought
misija mission
Mislim da... I think that...
misliti think
miš mouse
mišić muscle; **mišići** muscles
mitraljez machine gun
mlad young
mlad mesec new moon
mlada bride
mladež mole *on skin*
mladica sprout
mladić teenager; boy
mladoženja bridegroom
mlađi junior
mlečni dairy *adjective*
mlekara dairy *noun*
mleko milk; **mleko u prahu** powdered milk
mleti to grind
mlin mill
mlinara flour mill
mnogi many
mnogo a lot; much
množenje multiplication
množiti (se) multiply
mobilni telefon; mobitel cell phone; mobile phone
močvara marsh; swamp
moć power
moća sauce
moći to be able
moda fashion
model model
modem modem
moderan modern

modrica bruise
Mogu... I can...; **Mogu li da jedem?** May I eat?
moguć probable; **Moguće je.** It is probable.
mogućnost possibility
moj my; mine
mokar wet
molba petition
molim (vas/te)! please!
moliti (se) to pray
molitva prayer
momak boyfriend
momenat moment
monarh monarch
monarhija monarchy
morati must; to have to
more sea
most bridge
motor engine
motor; motorcikl motorbike
mozak brain
možda maybe
mračan *adjective* dark
mrak darkness
mrav ant
mraz frost
mreža net; **ribarska mreža; mreža za ribolov** fishing net; **mreža protiv komaraca** mosquito net
mršav *adjective* lean
mrtav dead
mrviti to grind
mrzeti to hate
mržnja hate
mu him
mučenik martyr
mučenje torture
mučiti to torture
mudar wise
mudrost wisdom
municija ammunition; munitions
munja lightning
muzika music; **narodna/ folklorna muzika** folk music

c = hi*ts*   č = *ch*urch   ć = *ty/chy*   d = *dy*   dž = *j*am

musliman/muslimanka Muslim
person
mušica fly
muškarac *noun* male
muški *adjective* male
muzej museum
muzički festival music festival
muzika music
muž man; husband
mužjak male *animal*

N

na to; for; on; **na primer** for
example; **na vreme** on time;
na crno black market
nabaviti to supply
nacionalnost nationality
način way; manner
naći to find
nada hope
nadimak nickname
nadvladati to conquer
nadzirati to control
nadzornik surveyor
nafta oil; **brod za prevoz nafte**
oil tanker; **rafinerija nafte** oil
refinery
naftovod oil pipeline
nag naked
nagib slope
naglo rapidly
nagnuti se to lean
nagrada prize
najamnik mercenary
najbolji best
najmlađe dete youngest child
najviše most
nakit jewelry
naknada pay; compensation
nama us
namera intention
nameravati to intend
namestiti to fix
nameštaj furniture
nana mint
naočari glasses; spectacles;

naočari za sunce sunglasses
napad attack; raid; invasion;
napad iz zasede hijacking
napadač iz zasede hijacker
napasti iz zasede to hijack
napasti to attack; to invade
napolje out
napolju outside
napor struggle
napraviti to make
napred forward(s); **napred!**
come in!
napredak progress
napuniti to load
nar pomegranate
narandžast orange *color*
naredba order; command
narediti; naređivati to order; to
command
narkoman drug addict
narod people; nation
narodna baština folklore
narodna igra folk dancing
narodna muzika folk music
narodni national
naručiti to order a meal
narukvica bracelet
nas us; ourselves
nasilje violence
nasip dam
nastaviti to continue; **nastavite!**
don't stop!
nastavnik school teacher
naš our
natezač spanner; wrench
natovariti to load
naučiti napamet to learn by
heart
naučni scientific
naučnik scientist
nauka science
navesti to state
navijati to wind
nažalost unfortunately
ne no; not; **ne još** not yet
nebo sky
nedaleko nearby

h = lo*ch*/*h*it   j = *y*et   š = *sh*ip   ž = a*z*ure

nećak

nećak nephew *brother's son*
nećaka niece *brother's daughter*
nedavno recently
nedelja Sunday
nedelja week
nedeljno weekly
nedostatak lack; shortage
nega care
negde somewhere; anywhere
nego than
negodovati to protest
nekako somehow
neki some
neko someone; anyone
nekoliko some; several
nekuvan uncooked
neljubazan unfriendly
nema problema! no problem!
Nemac German *male*
Nemačka Germany
nemački German *language/thing*
Nemica German *female*
nemoguć impossible
nemoj(te)...! do not...!; nemojte da stajete! don't stop!
neophodan necessary; neophodno je it's necessary
neoporeziv tax-free
neoženjen single *not married*
nepametan unwise
nepismen illiterate
neplodan arid
nepogoda disaster
nepotpun incomplete
nepoznat unknown
neprijatelj enemy
neprijateljski raspoložen unfriendly
neprilika trouble; inconvenience
nepromišljen unwise; thoughtless
nerazuman insane
nered riot
nerv nerve
neslan saltless

nesposobnost disability
nesreća accident
nesrećan unhappy; unfortunate
nestati to run out (of); Nestala je struja. The electricity has been cut off.
nešto something
neučtiv rude
neudata single *not married*
neudoban uncomfortable
neugodan uncomfortable
neumerenost excess
neuredan disorderly
neuspeh failure
nevažan insignificant
nevin innocent
nevolja trouble
nezakonit illegal
nezaposlen unemployed
nezaposlenost unemployment
nezavisan independent; nezavisna država independent state
nezavisnost independence
nežan smooth
nigde nowhere
nijansa shade *of color*
nijedan none
nikad never
niko nobody; none
ništa nothing; none
niti... niti neither ... nor
nivo *noun* level
niz range
nizak low; nizak krvni pritisak low blood pressure
noć night
noćna mora nightmare
noćni čuvar nightguard
noćni klub nightclub
noga leg
nokat nail *of finger/toe*
nokti fingernail
normalan normal
Norveška Norway
nos nose
nosač girder

c = hi*ts*   č = *ch*urch   ć = ty/chy   d = dy   dž = *j*am

nosila *hospital* stretcher
nositi to carry; to wear
nov new
nova godina New Year
novac money
novčana jedinica currency
novčanica bank note
novčanik wallet
novčić coin
novembar November
Novi Zeland New Zealand
novinar journalist
novine newspaper; **dnevne novine** daily newspaper; **engleske novine** newspaper in English
novogodišnja proslava New Year celebration
novorođenče newborn child
novosti news
nož knife
nula nought; zero
nužda necessity
nuždi: izlaz u nuždi emergency exit

NJ

nje her
njega him
njegov his; its; him
njemu him
njen her; hers; its
njih them; themselves
njihov their; theirs
njima them
njoj; nju her

O

o about; **o Jugoslaviji** ...about Yugoslavia
oba both
obala shore; coast
obaveza duty; obligation
obezbediti to supply
obezbeđenje security
običaj custom

običan ordinary
obično usually
obim volume; size
objasniti to explain
objašnjenje explanation; **objašnjenja** explanations
objava declaration
objaviti to publish
oblačiti to dress; **oblačiti se** to get dressed
oblak cloud
oblast area; district; province
oblik shape
obmanuti to mislead
obom yourself
obraz cheek
obrazovanje education
obrok meal
obrva eyebrow; **obrve** eyebrows
obućar cobbler
obući se to put on *clothes*
obuhvatiti to grasp
oburvavanje landslide
obustava rada strike *from work*
očekivati to expect
očevi fathers
oči eyes
očigledan evident
očuh stepfather
od of; since; than; **od ponedeljka** since Monday
odakle? where from?
odavno long ago
odbraniti to defend
odeća clothes
odeljenje department
odelo suit *of clothes*
odgovarajući suitable
odgovor answer
odgovoriti to answer
odigrati to perform
odjednom suddenly
odlasci departures
odlazak departure
odličan excellent
odlika distinction
odlomak extract

odlučiti to decide
odluka decision
odmah immediately
odmarati (se) to rest
odmor holidays; rest; break
odneti to take away
odnos relationship
odoleti to resist
održa(va)ti to maintain
odsutnost absence
odupreti se to resist
oduzeti to subtract
oduzimanje subtraction
odvijač wrench; spanner
odvod drain
oficir *military* officer
ofinger *clothes* hanger
oglas advert; ad
oglasiti to advertise
ogledalo mirror
ograda fence
ogranak branch
ograničenje limit
ograničiti to limit
ogrlica necklace
ogrtač overcoat
okačiti to hang
okanuti se quit
okean ocean
okliznuti se to slip
oko eye; about; **oko 50 milja** about 50 miles
okrenuti to turn
okretati to twist
okretnica roundabout *in road*
okrugao round
okrutan cruel
okružiti to surround
oktobar October
okupacione snage occupying forces
okupirati to occupy *a country*
olakšanje relief aid
olakšati to ease
olovka pen
olovo lead *metal*
oluja storm

on he
ona she
onda then
onesposobljen *adjective* disabled
oni they; those
opasač belt
opasan dangerous; severe
opasnost danger
opeći se to get burnt; to burn
opekotina *medical* burn; **sunčana opekotina** sunburn
operacija operation; **hirurška operacija** surgery; operation
operaciona sala operating theater/room
operater operator
opet again
opijum opium
opisati to describe
Opljačkan sam! I've been robbed!
opljačkati rob
oporezovati to tax
opozicija opposition
opran washed
oprema equipment
oprezan careful
oprezno! carefully!
opreznost caution
oprostiti to forgive
opsada siege
opseg range
opšti *adjective* general
opština town hall
optužba: Koja je optužba? What is the charge?
optužiti to accuse
opustiti se to relax
orah nut
orao eagle
orati to plow
organ organ *of body*
organizacija organisation
originalan original
ormarić cabinet; cupboard
oružje weapon; arms

c = hi*ts*   č = *ch*urch   ć = *ty/chy*   d = d*y*   dž = *j*am

osa wasp
osam eight
osamdeset eighty
osamnaest eighteen
osećati to feel
osetljiv sore
osica wasp
osiguranje insurance; **Imam osiguranje za imovinu.** My possessions are insured.; **Imam zdravstveno osiguranje.** I have medical insurance.
osim apart from; except; **osim toga** besides
oskudica poverty
osloboditi to free
osnova base
osnovati to establish
osoba person
osoblje staff
ostatak rest; remainder
ostati to stay
ostvariti to realize
osuditi to condemn
osvetliti to light
osvetljen illuminated
osvojiti to seize
osvrt review *article*
oštar sharp
otac father
otadžbina homeland
oteti to kidnap
oticati to swell
otići to leave
otkazati to cancel; **Let je otkazan.** The flight is canceled.
otkriti to discover
otmica kidnapping
otok swelling
otpor opposition
otpustiti to sack; to dismiss
otrov poison
otrovan septic
otvarač za flaše bottle opener; corkscrew
otvarač za konzerve can opener
otvoren *adjective* open

otvoriti to open
ovaj this
ovan ram
ovca sheep; ewe
ovčar shepherd; sheepdog
ovčetina mutton
ovde here
ove godine this year
ove nedelje this week
overiti to stamp a document
ovi these
ovoliko this much
ozbiljan serious; **Situacija je ozbiljna.** The situation is serious.
označiti to sign
oznaka mark
Oženjen sam. I am married. *said by a man*

P

pacijent *medical* patient
pacov rat
pad fall
Pada kiša. It is raining.
padina slope
padobran parachute
pahulje snowflakes
pakao hell
paket parcel; packet
palac thumb
palata palace
pamćenje memory
pametan intelligent
pamflet pamphlet
pankreas pancreas
pansion hostel; pension
pantalone trousers
papagaj parrot
papirnate maramice *paper* tissues
paprika pepper *vegetable*
par item
paradajz tomato
paralizovan paralyzed
paralizovati (se) to paralyze
parče piece

h = lo*ch*/hit   j = yet   š = *sh*ip   ž = a*z*ure

parfem perfume
park park
parking car park; parking lot
parkirati (se) to park
parlament parliament
partija *political* party
pas dog
pasoš passport; **broj pasoša** passport number
pasta za zube toothpaste
pasti to fall; to fall over; **pasti ispit** to fail an exam; **pasti na pamet** to happen
pastir shepherd
pastorka daughter *of wife's first husband*
pasulj beans
pašenog brother-in-law *wife's sister's husband*
patent zipper
patka duck
patrola patrol
pauk spider
paun peacock
pauza break; pause
pažljiv careful
pažljivo! carefully!
pčela bee
pečat *official* stamp
pečenje roast *of meat*
peć stove; heating stove
pećina cave
pedeset fifty
pedijatar pediatrician
pedijatrija pediatrics
pegla iron *for clothes*
pekara bakery
pekmez jam
pelcovati to vaccinate
pelena nappy; diaper; **Moram da promenim bebi pelene.** I need to change my baby's diaper.
pena za brijanje shaving cream
penicilin penicillin
penjati se to climb
period period *of time*

peron *railway* platform
perorez penknife
pesak sand
pesma song; poem
pesnik poet
pešačenje hiking
pešak pedestrian
peške on foot
peškir towel
pet five
peta heel
petak Friday
petao rooster
peticija petition
petnaest fifteen; **petnaest minuta** quarter of an hour
pevati to sing
piće drink
pijaca vegetable market
pijan drunk
piknik picnic
pile chicken
piletina chicken *meat*
piljar greengrocer
pilot pilot
pilula pill
pirinač rice
pisac writer
pisaća mašina typewriter
pisaći pribor stationery
pisanje writing
pisati to write
pištolj pistol
pitanje question
pitati to ask; **pitati za savet** to consult
piti to drink
pitom tame
pivo beer
plafon ceiling
plakati to cry; to weep
planina mountain
planinska reka mountain stream
planinski prolaz mountain pass
plastika plastic
plata pay
platiti to pay

c = hi*ts*   č = *ch*urch   ć = t*y*/*chy*   d = d*y*   dž = *j*am

platno cloth; material
plav blue
plavi patlidžan aubergine; eggplant
pleme clan
ples dance
plesanje dancing
plesti to knit
pletenica braid
plih boil
plivanje swimming
plivati to swim
plodan fertile
pluća lungs
plug plow
pluta cork *material*
pljačka robbery
pljačkaš robber
pljačkati to loot
pljunuti to spit
pljusak shower *of rain*
pljuvačka saliva
po about; according to; after; **po gradu** about town
pobeći to escape
pobeda victory
pobediti to beat; to win; **Ko je pobedio?** Who won?
poboljšati to improve
početak beginning
početak origin
početi to begin
pod ground; floor; under
podeliti to divide
podići to lift; to raise *prices etc.*
podlaktica forearm
podloga mat
podmetač mat
podne noon
podpredsednik vice-president *of country*
područje region
područje territory
podrum cellar
podstanar tenant
podučavanje instruction; teaching
podzemni underground

poezija poetry
poglavlje chapter
pogled view
pogodan appropriate; suitable
pogoditi to score *in sports*
pogodnost usefulness
pogrešiti to make a mistake
pogrešno wrong
pogubiti to execute
pohvala praise
pojačanje reinforcements
pojas belt
pojaviti se to appear
pojedinačan single
pokazati: Pokažite mi put do... Can you give me directions to...
poklon present; gift
pokoriti to conquer
pokrivač quilt
pokupiti to collect
pokušati to try
pokvaren rotten
pokvarenost corruption
pokvariti to spoil; **pokvariti se** to break down; **Pokvarila su nam se kola.** Our car has broken down.
pol sex *gender*
pola half; **pola sata** half-hour
polako! slowly!
polica cupboard; shelf
policajac policeman
policija police
policijska stanica police station
političar politician
politički political
politika politics
polna bolest venereal disease
polovan secondhand
položaj position
položiti to lay (down); **položiti ispit** to pass an exam
poluga lever
polugođe half year *school*
polusestra half-sister

h = lo*ch*/*h*it   j = *y*et   š = *sh*ip   ž = a*z*ure

poljana

poljana *noun* plain
polje field
poljoprivreda agriculture
poljoprivrednik farmer
poljubac kiss
pomeriti se to move
pomešati to mix
pomfrit french fries
pomiren reconciled
pomirenje reconciliation
pomoć help; **humanitarna pomoć** humanitarian aid
pomoći to help; **Možete li mi pomoći?/Molim vas pomozite mi.** Can you help me?; **upomoć!** help!
pomorandža orange *fruit*
ponašanje behavior
ponedeljak Monday
ponekad sometimes
poni pony
poništiti to undo
ponoć midnight
ponos pride
ponosan proud
ponoviti to repeat
ponovo again
poplava flood
popodne afternoon; **danas popodne** this afternoon
popraviti to fix; to repair
popravka repair
populacija population
popuniti formular to fill in a form
Poranio je. He is early.
porasti to grow up
poraz failure; defeat
poraziti to defeat
poražen defeated
porcelan chinaware
porcija portion
pored *adverb* besides
pored by; **pored toga** *preposition* besides
poredak order; arrangement

poreklo origin
porez *noun* tax
porodica family
poroditi se to give birth
portabilni televizor portable T.V.
portret portrait
poruka message
porušiti demolish
posao work; job; business
posavetovati se to consult
poseban separate; extra
posebno especially; separately
posedovati to own
posetilac visitor
posetiti to visit
posinak stepson
poslati to send
posle after; afterwards; **posle podne** p.m.
poslednji last; final
poslepodne afternoon
poslovan čovek businessman
poslovica proverb
poslovna žena businesswoman
poslovnica office
poslužavnik tray
posmatrač observer
pospan sleepy
posramljen ashamed
posrednik negotiator
postati to become
postava lining *of clothes*
postaviti to place
posteljica placenta
postići go to score a goal
postrojenje plant *industrial*
pošta mail; post office
poštanska marka *postal* stamp
poštansko sanduče mailbox
poštom by post
poštovanje respect
potkivati to shoe *a horse*
potkrovlje loft
potok stream

c = hi*ts*   č = *ch*urch   ć = *ty/chy*   d = *dy*   dž = *j*am

potonuti to sink
potpis signature
potreba necessity
potreba need
potres shock; concussion
potučen beaten
potvrda *proof of* receipt
povećati to raise *prices etc.*
povezati to connect
povlačiti se to retreat
povraćati to vomit
povratiti to undo
povratna karta return ticket
povrće vegetables
povreda hurt; injury
povreda *noun* hurt; injured
povrediti to hurt; to injure
povređen hurt; injured
povremeno occasionally
pozajmiti to borrow; to lend
poziv; pozivnica call; invitation
pozivni broj za inostranstvo international code
poznanik acquaintance
poznanstvo acquaintance
poznat famous
pozorišni komad *theater* play
pozorište theater
pozornica *theater* stage
pozvati to phone; to invite
požar fire; blaze
Požuri(te)! hurry up!!
prababa great-grandmother
pradeda great-grandfather
prah powder
prasak detonation
prase pig
prasnuti to detonate
prašak powder; **prašak za pranje** washing powder; detergent
prati to wash
pratilac companion
pratiti to follow

praunuk great-grandson
prav; pravo right; straight
prava rights; **prava žena** women's rights
pravda justice
pravi right; correct
pravilnik code *regulations*
pravilo law; rule; regulation
pravnik lawyer
pravna profesija legal profession
prazan *adjective* empty
praziluk gandana *leek*
praznik holiday
prazniti to empty
pre before; ago; **pre nedelju dana** a week ago
preći to go *over there*; to pass; to cross
predaja prtljaga check-in
predajnik transmitter
predati to submit; **predati se** to surrender
predavač professor
predavanje lecture
predavati to transmit
predgrađe suburb
predlog proposal
predmet subject
prednji; prednji deo front
predsednik president
predstava show
predstaviti to introduce
predstavljati to represent
predstavništvo consulate
preduzeće company; firm
pregled review
pregledati to examine *medically*
pregovarač negotiator
pregovaranje treaty
prehlada *medical* cold; **Imam prehladu.** I have a cold.
prekid recess; break
prekidač *electric* switch
prekjuče the day before yesterday

preko through; by means of; over; **preko reke** beyond the river

preksutra the day after tomorrow

prelom fracture

prema to; according to

premalo too little

premijer prime minister

preokrenuti to overturn

preostao spare

prepelica quail

prepisivati to copy *in class*

prepoznati to recognize

prepreka limit; **prepreka na putu** roadblock

presecanje intersection

presedati transfer flights

prestati to quit

presto throne

prestupna godina leap year

preteknuti; preticati to overtake *by car*

prevariti to mislead

prevazići to beat; to overcome

prevesti to translate

previše very; too (much/ many)

prevod translation

prevodilac translator

prevoz carriage

prevoziti to transport

prevrat revolution

prezime surname; family name

približan approximate

približno approximately

pribor set

priča story; tale

pričvrstiti to fasten

pridev adjective

prijatan nice

prijatelj *male* friend

prijateljica *female* friend

prijateljstvo friendship

prikaz representation

primer example; **na primer** for instance

primerak copy; item

primirje truce

primiti to receive

princ prince

princip principle

priprema preparation; **pripreme** preparations

pripremiti to prepare

priroda countryside; nature

prirodan natural; **prirodna bogatstva** natural resources; **prirodna nepogoda** natural disaster

pritisak pressure

pritisnuti to press

prizemljiti se to land *airplane*

prljav dirty

proći to pass; **proći ispit** to pass an exam

probati to taste

problem problem; **problem sa srcem; srčani problem** heart condition; **problem(i) sa varenjem** indigestion

probuditi se to wake up

proceniti to estimate

proces *legal* trial

procuriti to leak

prodaja karata ticket office

prodati to sell

prodavač shopkeeper; salesman

prodavačica saleswoman

prodavnica store; shop; **prodavnica cipela** shoe store; **prodavnica odeće** clothing shore

prodavnica pisaćeg pribora stationery store

produžiti lengthen

profesija profession

profesionalac professional *person*

profesor teacher

proglasiti to announce

program program; **kompjuterski program** computer program

progres progress

c = hi*ts*   č = *ch*ur*ch*   ć = ty/*chy*   d = d*y*   dž = *j*am

prohodan: Je li put prohodan? Is the road passable?
proizvod product
projektil missile
projektor projector
prolaz crossing
prolaznik passer-by
proleće spring *season*
proliv diarrhea
promašiti to miss
promena change
promeniti to change; **Želim da promenim dolare.** I want to change some dollars.
promet traffic
promrzline frostbite
propis regulation
propusnica pass; I.D.
prosečan *adjective* average
prosjak beggar
proslava party; celebration
proso millet
prostor area
prosuti to spill
prošli last; past; **prošle noći** last night; **prošle nedelje** last week; **prošle godine** last year
prošlost past *noun*
protest *noun* protest
protestovati to protest
proteza artificial limb; prothesis
protivnik opponent
protiv-vazdušna odbrana anti-aircraft force
protivzakonit disorderly
proveriti to check; **Proverite ulje.** Check the oil.
provesti vreme to spend time
provincija province
provizija commission; **Kolika je provizija?** What is the commission?
prozor window
prsluk waistcoat
prst finger; **prst na nozi** toe; **prsti** fingers

prsten ring
pršljen vertebra
prtljag luggage
prut stick
prvi first; **prva klasa** first class; **prva pomoć** first aid
pržiti to fry
psimo letter
psovati to swear; to curse
pšenica wheat
ptica bird
pucati to shoot; **Ne pucaj!** Don't shoot!
puder powder
pumpa pump; **pumpa za vodu** water pump
pumpati to pump; **pumpati vodu** to pump water
pun full; **pun mesec** full moon
puniti to fill
pupak navel
pupčana vrpca umbilical cord
purpuran purple
pustinja desert
pustiti to release
pušač smoker
pušenje smoking
pušiti (se) to smoke
puška gun; rifle; **puške** arms
put road; way
putanja track
puter butter
putna agencija travel agency
putni čekovi traveler's checks
putnik passenger; traveler; **putnici** passengers; travelers
putovanje *noun* travel
putovati to travel
puž snail

R

račun check/bill; receipt
računar computer
računica calculation
rad work; job
radar radar

h = lo*ch*/hit   j = yet   š = *sh*ip   ž = a*z*ure

radijator radiator

radio radio; **radio emisija** radio broadcast; **radio program** radio program; **radio stanica** radio station

raditi to do; to work; **Radim u banci.** I work in a bank.; **Telefon ne radi.** The phone doesn't work.

radni sto desk

radničko udruženje trade union

radnik worker

rafinerija refinery; **rafinerija nafte** oil refinery

ragbi rugby

raj paradise

rajsferšlus zipper

rak cancer; crab

raketa rocket

rame shoulder

rana wound

ranac backpack

ranije previously

raniti to wound

rano early

rapidan rapid

rapidno rapidly

rascepiti to split

rasejanje diaspora

raseljeno lice displaced person

rasipati to scatter

raskrsnica crossroads

raspon span

raspored timetable

rasprsnuti burst

rasprшiti to scatter

raspust school holidays

rastaviti to separate

rasti to grow

rasvetliti to light

rat war

ratni zarobljenik prisoner-of-war

ravan *adjective* level

ravnica *noun* plain

razbojnik robber

razdvajanje separation

razglednica postcard

razgovarati to talk

razgovor conversation

različit different

razlika difference

razlog putovanja reason for travel

razmak interval

razmatranje discussion

razmatrati to discuss

razmena exchange

razmirica feud

razmotriti to consider

razred *academic* class

razum reason; mind

razumeti to understand

razvezati to undo

razvod braka divorce

razvoj development

rđa rust

rebro rib; **rebra** ribs

recepcija reception *desk/ area*

recesija recess; break

reč word

rečenica sentence *of words*

rečit eloquent

rečna obala river bank

rečnik dictionary

reći to say; to tell

red row; line; queue; order

red vožnje travel timetable

reditelj: filmski reditelj filmmaker; **pozorišni reditelj** theater director

registracija car registration

reka river

reklama advert; ad

reklamirati to advertise

rekreacija recreation

relativan *adjective* relative

religija religion

rendgen X-rays

reportaža *news* story

reporter reporter

reprezentacija representation

reprezentativan typical

c = hi*ts*   č = *ch*urch   ć = *ty/chy*   d = *dy*   dž = *j*am

republika republic
rerna oven
restoran restaurant
rešiti to solve
revija review; magazine
revolucija revolution
revolver pistol
revolveraš gunman
rezervacija reservation *for ticket/room*
rezervisati to reserve; **Mogu li da rezervišem mesto?** Can I reserve a place/seat?
rezervna guma spare tire
rezervoar *petrol* tank; gas bottle/canister
rezultat result; score *in sports*; **Koji je rezultat?** What's the score?
režim regime
režiser theatre/film director
riba fish
ribarenje fishing
ribarska mreža fishing net
ribnjak pond
rizik risk
rizikovati to risk
riža rice
rob slave
robna kuća department store
roditelji parents
roditi to give birth to
rođak cousin; relative; **rođaci** relatives
rođen: Gde ste rođeni? Where were you born?; **Rođen/rođena sam u Njujorku.** I was born in New York.
rođendan birthday
rođenje birth
rog horn
rok period *of time*
roman novel
rosa dew
rotkvica radish
roze pink

rub hem
ručak lunch
ručka handle
ručna tašna handbag
ručni rad handicraft
rudar miner
rudnik mine *for minerals*
ruka hand; arm
rukav sleeve
rukavice gloves
rukovodilac president *of organisation*
rupa hole; puncture; flat tire
rupica za dugme buttonhole
Rus Russian *male*
Rusija Russia
ruski Russian *language/thing*
Ruskinja Russian *female*
ruševine ruins; rubble
ruta route
ruž za usne lipstick
ruža rose
rvanje wrestling

S

s; sa with; to; **čaj s mlekom** tea with milk; **sa strane** to the side; **Otišao/otišla sam sa njim.** I went with him.
sabiranje addition
sabrati *maths* to add
sačekaj(te) momenat! wait a moment!
S.A.D. U.S.A.
sad; sada now; **upravo sada** just now
sadašnji *adjective* present *time*
sadašnjost *noun* present *time*
saditi to plant
sadnica seedling
sadržavati to contain
saglasnost agreement
sahrana funeral
sajam show; fair
sakriti to hide; **sakriti se** to take shelter

sala hall; **sala za konferencije** conference room

salata salad

salo *noun* fat

salveta napkin

sam single; only; alone

samoposluga supermarket

san dream

sandale sandals

sanduk box; chest

sanjati to dream

saobraćaj traffic

saobraćajna policija traffic police

sapun soap

saradnja cooperation

sastanak meeting

sastav structure

sat hour; wristwatch; clock; **pola sata** half-hour; **Kolko ima sati?** What time is it?

satelit satellite

satelitski telefon satellite phone

sav all; entire; **sav svet** all the world

savet council

savetnik consultant

savez union

saviti to bend

savladati to overcome

savremen contemporary

savršen perfect

scena *theater* stage

se self

sebe self; himself; herself; myself

seckati to chop

seći to cut

sedam seven

sedamdeset seventy

sedamnaest seventeen

sedenje sitting

sedište seat

sednica session

sejati to sow

sekira ax

sekirica pickax

sekretar; sekretarica secretary

sekunda *noun* second

selo village

seljački sir cottage cheese

seljak villager

semafor traffic lights

seme grain; seeds

sendvič sandwich

senka shade; shadow

seno hay

septembar September

septičan septic

serija series: radio series

sesija session

sesti to sit

sestra sister; *female* cousin; **sestre** sisters

sestričina niece *sister's daughter*

sestrić nephew *sister's son*

setiti se to remember

setva planting

sever *noun* north

severan north(ern)

Severna Irska Northern Ireland

sezona season

sfera region

shvatiti to grasp

sida AIDS

siguran certain; safe

sigurno certainly

sigurnost safety

sijalica lightbulb

sijati to shine

sila force

silaziti to descend

silovanje rape

simbol symbol

simptom *medical* symptom

sin son

sinagoga synagogue

sinoć last night

sinovi sons

sintaksa syntax

sipati to pour

sir cheese

sirće vinegar

sirena car horn

c = hi*ts*   č = *ch*urch   ć = t*y/chy*   d = *dy*   dž = *j*am

siroče orphan

siromašan poor

siromaštvo poverty

sirotište orphanage

sirov raw

sirup syrup

sisar mammal

sisati to suck

sistem system

sit full up; **Ja sam sit!** I am full up!

situacija situation

siv grey

sjaj flash

Sjedinjene Američke Države (S.A.D.) United States of America

skakavac grasshopper

skijanje skiing

skijati to ski

skinuti to take off *something*

skladište store *for storage*

sklopiti mir to make peace

skočiti to jump

skorašnji *adjective* recent

skoro almost; recently

skrenuti to turn; **skreni(te) desno** turn right!; **skreni(te) levo** turn left!

skrhati to crash

skriven hidden

skroman modest

skrovište shelter

skup expensive

skupiti to collect

skupština parliament; assembly

skver square

slab weak

sladak *adjective* sweet

sladoled ice cream

slama straw

slan salty

slatkiš candy; sweet(s)

slaviti to celebrate

slavuj nightingale

sledeći next; **sledeće nedelje** next week

slep *adjective* blind; **slepi** blind people

slepi miš bat

sleteti to land *airplane*

sličan similar

slika picture; painting; photo

slikar painter

slikati to paint

sloboda freedom

slobodan free; liberated; **slobodna štampa** the free press; **slobodno vreme** free time; **Je li ovo mesto slobodno?** Is this seat free?

sloj section

slom *medical* shock

slomiti to crash; to fracture

slon elephant

slovo letter *of alphabet*; **slova** letters

složiti se to come to an agreement

slučaj accident

slučajno accidentally

sluga servant

slušalac listener

slušati to listen

služba office; service; **služba za informacije** information office

službenik office worker

smanjiti to decrease

smatrati to consider

smeće trash

smeh laughter

smejati se to laugh

smesa mixture

smešan funny

smeštaj accommodation

smešten situated

smisao sense; meaning

smrdeti to stink

smrt death

smrzavanje freezing

smrznuti to freeze

snaga strength

snaha; snaja sister-in-law

h = loch/hit   j = yet   š = ship   ž = azure

brother's wife; daughter-in-law

sneg snow; **Pada sneg.** It is snowing.

so salt

soba room

sočivo lens; lentils; **sočiva** contact lenses

soko hawk

sopstven *adjective* own

sos sauce

sova owl

spanać spinach

spasiti to save; to rescue

spavaća soba bedroom

spavati to sleep

specijalista specialist

spiker speaker

spisak list

spojnica girder

spoljašnjost *noun* outside

spomenik monument

spor contest; slow

sporazum formal agreement

sporedna ulica sidestreet

sporo! slowly!

sportista sportsman

sportovi sports

sposoban able

sposobnost ability

sprat floor; story

sprečiti to prevent

spreman ready; **Spreman sam.** I am ready.

spremiti to prepare

spustiti to lower

sramota shame

sramotiti to shame

srce heart; **problem sa srcem** heart condition

srčani problem heart condition

srčani udar heart attack

sreća luck

srećan happy

srebro silver

sreda Wednesday

sredina middle

srednja škola high school

srednji mid

sredstva komunikacije media

sredstvo protiv insekata insecticide

sresti to meet

srodstvo *blood* relationship

Srbija Serbia

Srbin/Srpkinja Serbian *male*

srpski Serbian *thing*

stadion stadium

stado herd; flock

stajati to stand

stakleno sočivo lens

staklo glass *substance*

stalan constant

stan apartment

stanar tenant

stani(te)! stop!

stanica station; **policijska stanica** police station

stanje position; state

stanovati to live; to dwell

stanovništvo population

star old

starac old man

stari ancient; **stari grad** old city

starica old woman

stariji *adjective* senior; **stariji brat** elder brother

starost age

statua statue

staviti to put

staza path

steći to gain

stena rock

stepen degree *grade*

stepenice stairs

stetoskop stethoscope

stići to reach; to arrive (at)

stisnuti to squeeze

sto hundred; table

stoka cattle

stolar carpenter

stolica chair

stoljnjak tablecloth

stomak stomach; **bol u stomaku** stomachache

stopa foot *measurement*

c = hi**ts**   č = *ch*urch   ć = ty/*chy*   d = dy   dž = *j*am

stopalo foot
strah fear
strahovati to fear
stran foreign
strana page; side
stranac stranger; foreigner
stranka client; *political* party
strašan terrible
stražar guard
stražariti to guard
stric uncle *father's brother*
strići to shear
strina aunt *father's brother's wife*
strog severe
strpljiv *adjective* patient; **Budi(te) strpljivi!** Be patient!
stršljen hornet
stručnjak specialist
struja electricity
struk waist
struktura structure
student student
studija; studiranje *academic* study
studiranje to study
stvar thing
stvaran real
stvarati to create
stvarnost reality
subota Saturday
sud; sudnica law court
sudbina destiny
sudija judge; referee
sudopera sink *basin*
suđenje *legal* trial
sukob fight
suma sum
sumnja doubt
sunce sun; **Greje sunce.** It is sunny.
sunčana opekotina sunburn
sunđer sponge
suočiti se sa to face
supa soup; **supa od povrća** vegetable shop
suprotan opposite

suprotnost opposition
suprug husband
sused neighbor
susnežica sleet
susret meeting
sutra tomorrow
suv dry
suvišan spare
suvo grožđe raisins
suza *noun* tear
svađa row; argument
svaka tri meseca quarterly
svakako *adverb* sure
svaki each; every; **svakog dana** daily; **svake nedelje** weekly; **svake godine** yearly
svastika sister-in-law *wife's sister*
sve all; everything
svečanost gala
sveća candle; **sveće** candles
svećnjak candlestick
svedočiti to testify
svedok witness
svekar father-in-law *to a bride*
svekrva mother-in-law *husband's mother*
sveska notebook; **sveska za vežbanje** exercise book
sveštenik priest
svet world
svetac saint
svetao light; bright
sveti holy
svetiljka torch; flashlight; **svetla (na kolima)** flashlight
svetlo bright *light*
svetlo; svetlost *noun* light
svež fresh *food*
svi everyone; **svi zajedno** all together
sviđati se to like; **Sviđa mi se...** I like...; **Ne sviđa mi se...** I don't like...
svila silk
svilen silken
svinjetina pork

h = lo*ch*/*h*it   j = *y*et   š = *sh*ip   ž = a*z*ure

svirati to play *a musical instrument*

svrab itch

svući se to get undressed

Š

šafran saffron

šah chess

šaka fist; handful

šakal jackal

šal scarf

šala joke

šalter cashier's booth

šampon shampoo

šanac trench

šargarepa carrot

šator tent

šav stitch

šećer sugar

šećerna bolest diabetes

šef boss; chief

šesnaest sixteen

šest six

šešir hat

šetati to walk

šezdeset sixty

šibice matches *for fire*

šifra code *number*

šiljak point; end

širiti to spread

širok wide

šišati to shear

šiti to sew

škola school; **srednja škola** high school

školjka *sea* shell

škorpija scorpion

Škotlanđanin/Škotlanđanka Scot

Škotska Scotland

škotski Scottish *language/ thing*

šljiva plum

šljunak gravel

šminka make-up; cosmetics

šofer chauffeur

šoferšajbna windscreen *car*

šok shock

šokiran astonished

šolja cup

Španac/Španjolka Spaniard

španski Spanish *language/thing*

špic traffic jam

špijun spy

šporet cooker; stove

špric syringe

šraf screw

šrafciger screwdriver

šrapnel shrapnel

šta? what?; **šta je to?** what's that?

šta god whatever; **Uzmite šta god želite.** Take whatever you want.

štab headquarters

štampa print; printing press

štampač printer *computer*

štamparija printer *place*

štampati to print

štap stick; walking stick

štaviše *preposition* besides

štene puppy

štetan harmful

što which

štrajk strike *from work*

štrajkovati to strike *from work*

šubara fur hat

šuma forest

šuma wood *forest*

šurak brother-in-law *wife's brother*

šuster cobbler

švercer smuggler

T

tabak hartije sheet *of paper*

taban sole

tabla blackboard

tableta tablet; **tablete za spavanje** sleeping pill(s)

tacna saucer

tačan *adjective* correct
tačan exact; proper
tačka item; stop
taj that
tajan *adjective* secret
tajna *noun* secret; **tajne** secrets
tajna policija secret police
tajni *adjective* underground
takav such
takmičenje competition
tako so
takođe too; also
taksi taxi
taktika tactic
tama darkness
tamo there
tanak thin
tanker oil tanker
tanjir plate
taoc hostage
tast father-in-law *to a groom*
tašna: ručna tašna handbag
tašta mother-in-law *wife's mother*
tavan loft
tavanica ceiling
teatar theater
tebe yourself *singular*
tečnost liquid
tehničar operator
tehnički technical
tehnika technique
tekst text
tele calf *animal*
telefon telephone; **javni telefon** pay-phone
telefonirati to phone
telegram telegram
telekomunikacije telecommunications
teleks telex
teleskop telescope
teletina veal
televizija television
televizijska serija T.V. series

televizijski kanal T.V. channel
telo body
temelj foundation *of building*
temperatura temperature
tempo pace
tenis tennis
tenk *military* tank
teoretski theoretical
teorija theory
tepih carpet
terasa veranda
teritorija territory
termin session
termit termite
termometar thermometer
test test
testament will *legal*
testenine pasta
testera saw
testirati to test
tetka aunt *father's/mother's sister*
težak heavy; difficult
težina weight
ti you *singular*
tih *adjective* quiet
tiho quietly
tikva pumpkin
tinejdžer teenager *boy*
tinejdžerka teenager *girl*
tipičan typical
tišina silence
tkanje weaving
tkati to weave
tkivo tissue
tlo ground; soil
to that; it
toalet toilet(s)
toalet papir toilet paper
točak wheel
tok flow
toliko so; so much/many
tona ton; tonne
top cannon
topao warm

toplomer thermometer
toranj tower
torba bag
tortura torture
tost toast *bread*
tovar cargo
tovarni konj packhorse
tradicija tradition
tradicionalan traditional
trafika newsstand
trag mark; track
traka tape; cassette
traktor tractor
transformator transformer
transfuzija transfusion; **transfuzija krvi** blood transfusion
transport transport
trauma trauma
trava grass; herb
tražiti to look for
trčati to run
trebati to need; **Treba mi...** I need...
treći third
trepavice eyelashes
tresti to shake
trešnja cherry
trg town square
trgovac salesman
trgovac trader
trgovkinja saleswoman
tri three
trideset thirty
trinaest thirteen
trka race; **konjske trke** horse racing
trljati to rub
trn thorn
trnokop pickax
tromboza thrombosis
tromesečnik quarterly magazine
tron throne
trošiti novac to spend money
trpezarija dining room
trudna pregnant; **Trudna sam.** I'm pregnant.

truo rotten
trup thorax
trupe troops
tržište market
tuberkuloza tuberculosis
tuce dozen
tuča fight
tući to beat
tuga sorrow
tumač interpreter
tumačiti to interpret
tunel tunnel
Turčin Turk *male*
turista tourist; **turisti** tourists
turistička agencija tourist office
turizam tourism
Turkinja Turk *female*
tuš shower *bath*
tuširanje *taking a* shower
tužan sad
tvoj your *informal singular*
tvoji yours *informal plural*
tvrd hard; not soft
tvrđava castle

U

u in; into; to; **u korist...** for the sake of; **u toku** during; **u zemlji** in the country
ubijanje; ubistvo killing
ubiti to kill
ubosti to sting
učenik school pupil
učenje to study
učestvovati to participate
učitelj school teacher
učiti to learn; to teach
učtiv polite
ući to go in; **ući u vozilo** to get into a vehicle
udaljen distant
udar shock; *medical* concussion; **električni udar** electric shock

udariti to hit; **udariti pečat** to stamp a document

Udata sam. I am married *said by a woman*

udoban comfortable; **Ovo sedište je udobno.** This car seat is comfortable.

udovac widower

udovi (tela) limbs (of body)

udovica widow

udruženje union

udvostručiti to double

uđite! come in!

ubica killer

ugalj coal; charcoal

ugao corner

uglavnom generally

ugodan comfortable

ugovor contract

ugriz zmije snakebite

uhapsiti to take prisoner

uho ear

ujak uncle *mother's brother*

ujed zmije snakebite

Ujedinjene Nacije United Nations

ujesti to bite

ujna aunt *mother's brother's wife*

uključen included

uključiti to switch on

ukratko briefly

ukrcati se to board *a plane*

ukus taste

ukusan tasty

ulaz entrance

ulica street

uliti to infuse

uložak sanitary towel; **ulošci** sanitary towels

ulje oil

um mind

umesto instead

umešan skilled

umetnik artist

umetnost art

umnjak wisdom tooth

umoran tired

umoriti to tire; **umoriti se** to get tired

umotati to roll up

umreti to die

unazad backwards

unca ounce

uniforma uniform

uniformisan uninformed

unihop čarape tights

uništiti to destroy

univerzitet university

unuk grandson

unuka granddaughter

unutar inside

unutrašni; unutarnji internal

unutrašnji; unutarnji *adjective* interior

unutrašnjost *noun* interior

uobičajen normal

upaliti to light; **upaliti vatru** to light a fire

upaljač lighter

upaljen switched on

upaljiv inflammable

uplašiti frighten

upomoć! help!

uporediti compare

uprava organisation; administration

upravljač administrator

upravljanje direction

upravljati to direct

upravni administrative

upravnik manager

upravo sada just now

uputstva manual *book*

uputstvo instructions *for use*

urednik editor

uređenje; uređivanje arrangement

urin urine

uskoro soon

uslov condition; term

usna lip
uspeh success
uspomena memory
uspostaviti to establish
uspravan upright
usta mouth
ustanoviti to establish
ustati to get up
ustav constitution
uši ears
ušivanje stitching
ušivati to stitch
uštedeti to save *money*
utakmica match *football*
uterus uterus
utikač *electric* plug
utorak Tuesday
utroba guts
utvrđenje fort
uvek always
uvesti to import
uvo ear
uvoziti to import
uvrnut twisted
uvući to put in
uz *adverb* besides; **uz to** *preposition* in addition to
uzak narrow
uzbuna emergency
uzeti to take
uzjahati to mount *a horse*
uzložba exhibition
uzorak model; sample
uzrok reason; cause
uzrokovati to cause
uživo live broadcast

V

vađenje krvi blood test
vakcina vaccination
vakcinisati to vaccinate
vama yourselves
van out
variti to brew
vas yourselves
vaš your *plural;* your *formal singular*

vaši yours *formal plural;* lice
vata cotton wool
vatra fire
vazduh air
vazdušna snaga air force
vazdušni napad air-raid
vazdušni pravac airline
važan important; **Nije važno.** It doesn't matter!
važnost importance
večan eternal
veče evening
večera supper
večeras this evening; tonight
već already
većina majority
većina most
vegetarijanski vegetarian
vek century
vekna hleba loaf
veličina size
velika količina a lot
veliki big; large; great
vena vein
venčanje wedding
venerična bolest venereal disease
ventilator fan *electric*
vepar boar
vera faith
veranda veranda
veroispovest religion
verovatan probable
verovati to believe
verovatno probably
verovatnoća probability
verska sekta religious sect
vesti news
veš za pranje laundry
vešalica *clothes* hanger
vešernica laundry (place)
vešt skilled
veštački artificial; **veštačka noga** artificial leg; **veštačka ruka** artificial arm; **veštačko oko** artificial eye; **veštačko**

đubrivo fertilizer
veština skill
vetar wind
veto veto
vetrobran windshield
vetrovit windy
veverica squirrel
vez embroidery
veza relationship
vezati to tie
vežbanje exercise; activity
vi you *plural*
vid sight; eyesight
video video; video player
video kamera camera
video kaseta video cassette
videti to see
vikati to shout
vikend weekend
vilica jaw
vilinski konjic dragonfly
viljuška fork
vino wine
vinova loza vine
virus virus; **kompjuterski virus** computer virus
visina height
visok tall; high; **visok krvni pritisak** high blood pressure; **visoka stručna sprema** *academic* degree
visoko high
višak excess
više more; **više manje** more or less; **više od toga** more than that; **više voleti** to prefer
viši *adjective* senior
višnja cherry
vitamini vitamins
viza visa
vlada government
vladati to rule
vlaga damp
vlakno thread
vlasnik owner; **vlasnik zgrade** landlord

vlasništvo ownership
vlast power
vlastit *adjective* own
vlastodržac ruler *person*
vlažan wet; damp; humid
vo ox
voće fruit
voćni sok fruit juice
voćnjak orchard
voda water; **voda za piće** drinking water; **mineralna voda** mineral water; **vruća voda** hot water
vodenica watermill
vodič guide; leader; guidebook
voditelj speaker *on radio, etc.*
voditi rat to wage war
voditi to guide; to lead
vodopad waterfall
vođa head; boss
vojni *adjective* military; **vojna baza** military base; **vojna obaveza** military service; **vojni puč** coup d'etat
vojnik soldier
vojska army
volan steering wheel
voleti to like; to love; **Volim...** I like...; **Ne volim...** I don't like...
volja will; willpower
voz train
vozač driver
vozačka dozvola car papers; driver's license
voziti to drive
vrabac sparrow
vrana crow
vrat neck
vrata door
vratiti to return; to reverse
vrč mug
vreća bag; **vreća za spavanje** sleeping bag
vredeti to be worth
vreme time; weather; **provesti**

vreme to pass time; **dugo vreme** for a long time; **na vreme** on time; **slobodno vreme** free time; **u isto vreme** at the same time; **za vreme** during

vreti to boil

vrh top

vrlo very

vrsta kind; type

vršiti to perform

vruć hot; **vruća voda** hot water; **Vruće je./Vrućina je.** It is hot.; **Vruće mi je./Vrućina mi je.** I am hot.

vrućina heat

vučenje: konopac za vučenje tow rope

vući to pull

vuk wolf

vuna wool

vunen woolen

Z

za for; **za vreme** during

zabeleške notes

zaboraviti to forget

zaboravljen forgotten

zabrana veto

zabraniti to forbid; to veto

zabranjen forbidden; **zabranjen ulaz** no entry; **zabranjeno pušenje** no smoking

zabrinut worried; **biti zabrinut** to be worried

zaceliti to heal

začin herb; spice

začuđen astonished

zadatak: domaći zadatak homework

zadovoljan satisfied

zadovoljavajući satisfactory

zadovoljstvo pleasure

zaduženo lice *noun* official

zaglaviti to stick *something*

zagrejati to heat

zahvalan grateful; **Zahvalan sam.** I am grateful.

zahvaliti (se) to thank

zainteresovati to interest

zaista indeed

zajedno together

zakašnjenje delay

zaklati to slaughter

zakleti se to swear an oath

zaklon shade; protection

zakloniti se to take shelter

zaključati to lock

zaključujući *adjective* final

zakočiti to brake

zakon law

zakonit legal; **zakonito pravo** legal right

zakopati to bury

zalazak sunca sunset

zalepiti to stick

zalihe supplies

zalogaj snack

zameniti to replace

zamka trap

zamotati wrap

zamrznuti to freeze

zanatlija craftsman

zanimanje job; occupation; profession

zanimljiv interesting

zaoštriti to sharpen

zapad *noun* west

zapadni west(ern)

zapaliti vatru to light a fire

zapis inscription

zapremina volume; size

zapušač *bath* plug; cork

zarada earrings

zaraditi to earn

zarasti to heal

zaraza infection; epidemic

zaražen infected

zarobiti to take prisoner; to take hostage

zasaditi to plant

zaseda ambush

zaspati to go to sleep

zastoj stop
zaštita protection
zaštititi to protect
zašto why
zatišje ceasefire
zato (što) because
zaturiti to lose; to mislay
zatvor prison; constipation; **Imate li zatvor?** Are you constipated?
zatvorenik prisoner
zatvoreno closed
zatvoriti to close; **zatvoriti vrata** to close a door
zauzet busy
zavesa curtain
zavežljaj package
zavijati to wind
zaviti to roll up
zavoj bandage; dressing
završen complete
završiti to finish
zavrtati to twist
zbog because of
zbuniti to confuse
zbunjen confused; dizzy
zdela dish
zdrav healthy
zdravlje health
zdravo! hello!
zdravstveno osiguranje medical insurance
zdravstvo healthcare
zebeležiti to record
zec rabbit; hare
zelen green; **zelena salata** lettuce
zemlja earth; land; country
zemljište garden; plot
zemljotres earthquake
zenica pupil *of eye*
zet son-in-law; brother-in-law *sister's husband*
zglob wrist; joint
zgodan useful
zgrabiti to seize
zgrada building
zid wall

zidar builder
zihernadla safety pin
zima winter
zlato gold
zlo evil; **dobro i zlo** good and evil
zločin crime
zločinac criminal
zmaj kite
zmija snake; **ugriz zmije; ujed zmije** snakebite
značajan important
značajnost importance
značenje meaning
znak sign; road sign
znan known
znanje knowledge
znati to know; **Znam.** I know.; **Ne znam.** I don't know.; **Da li znate njega/nju?** Do you know him/her?
znoj sweat
zoološki vrt zoo
zora dawn
zreo ripe
zrno grain
zub tooth; **zubi** teeth
zubar dentist
zubobolja toothache
zvaničan *adjective* official
zvaničnik official; **zvaničnici** officials
zvanje profession
zvati to call; **Zovite policiju!** Call the police!
zvezda star; **zvezde** stars
zviždati to whistle
zvoniti to ring *a bell*
zvono bell
zvuk sound

Ž

žaba frog
žalba complaint
žaliti se to complain
žao mi je! sorry!
ždrebac stallion

h = lo*ch*/*h*it   j = *y*et   š = *sh*ip   ž = a*z*ure

žedan thirsty; **Žedan sam.** I'm thirsty.

žeđ thirst

žele jelly

želeti to want; **Želim...** I want...; **Ne želim...** I don't want...; **Želim šišanje.** I want a haircut.

železnica railway

železnička stanica railway station

žena woman; wife; **žene** women

ženka noun female for animals

ženski adjective female

žeti to harvest

žetva harvest

žica wire; string

žig official stamp

žila vein

žilavo meso tough meat

žilet razor blade

živ alive

živac nerve

živeti to live

živina livestock; poultry

život life

životinja animal; **domaća životinja** domestic animal; **životinje** animals

životni stil way of life

žmigavac indicator light

žrtva victim; **žrtve** victims; **žrtve zemljotresa** victims of an earthquake

žuč gall bladder

Žurim. I'm in a hurry.

žurka party; celebration

žut yellow

žutica hepatitis

žvakaća guma chewing gum

žvakati to chew

ENGLISH—SERBIAN
ENGLESKI—SRPSKI

A

ability sposobnost
able sposoban; **to be able** moći
about o; oko; po; **about Yugoslavia** o Jugoslaviji; **about 50 miles** oko 50 milja; **about town** po gradu
above iznad
absence odsutnost
academy akademija
accident slučaj; nesreća
accidentally slučajno
accommodation smeštaj
according to prema; po
accuse optužiti
acquaintance poznanstvo; poznanik
acre jutro; aker
adapter *electric* adapter
add dodati; *maths* sabrati
addition sabiranje
address adresa
adjective pridev
administration administracija; *organisation* uprava
administrative upravni; izvršni
administrator izvršitelj; upravljač
advantage korist
advert oglas; *T.V./radio commercial* reklama
advertise oglasiti; reklamirati
after po; posle
afternoon popodne; poslepodene; **this afternoon** (danas) popodne
afterwards posle; kasnije
again opet; ponovo

age starost
ago pre; **a week ago** pre nedelju dana; **a while ago** nedavno; **a moment ago** malopre; **long ago** davno; odavno
agreement saglasnost; **formal agreement** sporazum; **to come to an agreement** složiti se
agriculture agrikultura; poljoprivreda
agronomist agronom
aid pomoć
AIDS sida
aim cilj
air vazduh
airbase aerodrom
air conditioner klima uređaj
airdrop izbaciti iz vazduha
airfield aerodrom
air force vazdušna snaga
airline vazdušni pravac
air mail letter avionsko pismo
airplane avion
airport aerodrom
air-raid vazdušni napad
alarm clock budilnik
alcohol alkohol
alight: *illuminated* osvetljen; *switched on* upaljen; **to be alight** *on fire* goreti
alive živ
all sve; **all together** svi zajedno; **all the world** sav svet; ceo svet
allergic alergičan
allow dozvoliti
almond badem
almost skoro

h = loch/hit   j = yet   š = ship   ž = azure

alone

alone sam

already već

also takođe

although iako

always uvek

ambassador ambasador

ambulance ambulanta

ambush zaseda; klopka

America Amerika

American *person* Amerikanac/Amerikanka; *thing* američki

ammunition municija

among među

amount količina; iznos

amputate amputirati

ancient stari; drevni

and i

anemia anemija

anesthetic anestezija; anestetik

angry ljut

animal životinja; **animals** životinje

ankle članak

anniversary godišnjica

annual godišnji

another drugi; **Another bottle, please!** Još jednu flašu, molim!

answer *noun* odgovor; *verb* odgovoriti

ant mrav

anti-aircraft force protivvazdušna odbrana

antibiotic antibiotik

anti-freeze antifriz

antiseptic antiseptik

anyone neko; bilo ko

anywhere negde; bilo gde

apart from *separately* posebno; *except* osim; izuzev

apartment stan

appear pojaviti se

appetite apetit

apple jabuka

appropriate *suitable* pogodan

approximately približno

apricot kajsija

April april

architect arhitekta

argument *row* svađa

area prostor; oblast

arid suv; neplodan

arm ruka

armored car blindirana kola

arms puške; oruzje

army vojska; armija

arrangement uređivanje; uređenje; **arrangements** *deals* dogovori

arrest hapšenje

arrive stići

arsenal arsenal

art umetnost

artery arterija

artificial veštački; **artificial limb** proteza; **artificial leg** veštačka noga; **artificial arm** veštačka ruka; **artificial eye** veštačko oko

artillery artiljerija

artist umetnik

ashamed posramljen

Asia Azija

ask pitati

asleep: to fall asleep zaspati; to be asleep spavati

aspirin aspirin

assassin ubica

assassination atentat

assault napad

assembly *government* skupština

asthma astma

astonished začuđen; šokiran

at kod

atheist ateista

athletics atletika

atomic atomski

attack napad; *verb* napasti

aubergine plavi patlidžan

aunt *father's/mother's sister* tetka; *father's brother's wife* strina; *mother's brother's wife* ujna

c = hi*ts*   č = *ch*urch   ć = *ty/chy*   d = *dy*   dž = *j*am

Australia Australija
Australian *person* Austra-lijanac/Australijanka; *thing* australijski
author autor
autumn jesen
avalanche lavina
average *adjective* prosečan
aversion averzija
aviation avijacija
awake budan; **to be awake** budan
ax sekira

B

baby beba
back *noun* leđa
backache bol u leđima
backpack ranac
backwards unazad; **to go backwards** ići unazad
bacteria bakterija
bad loš
badly loše
bag torba; vreća
baggage prtljag
bakery pekara
balcony balkon
ball lopta
ballpoint pero
banana banana
bandage *medical* zavoj
Band-Aid *plaster* flaster; hanzaplast
bandit bandit
bank banka
banker bankar
bar bar
barbed wire bodljikava žica
barber berberin
barefoot bos
bark *verb* lajati
barley ječam
barrel *storage* bure; *of gun* cev
base *bottom* osnova; **military base** vojna baza

basin lavabo
basis osnova
basket korpa; koš
basketball košarka
bat slepi miš
bathe kupati (se)
bathroom kupatilo
battery *electric* baterija
battle bitka
bayonet bajonet
be biti; *and see page 26.*
beam *girder* greda
beans pasulj; **green beans** boranija
bear medved
beard brada
beat tući; *to overcome* prevazići; *to win* pobediti
beaten potučen
beautiful lep
beauty lepota
because zato (što); **because of** zbog
become postati
bed krevet; **to go to bed** ići u krevet
bedroom spavaća soba
bee pčela
beef govedina
beer pivo
beet; beetroot cvekla
before pre
beggar prosjak
begin početi
beginning početak
behavior ponašanje
behind iza
belief vera; uverenje
believe verovati
believer vernik; pristalica
bell zvono
below ispod
belt pojas; kaiš; opasač; **cartridge belt** opasač
bench klupa
bend *verb* saviti
berry bobica

h = lo*ch*/*hi*t   j = yet   š = *sh*ip   ž = a*z*ure

besides *adverb* uz; pored; osim; *preposition* uz to; pored toga; osim toga; takođe; štaviše

best najbolji

better bolji; **I feel better.** *health* Bolje se osećam.

between između

beyond *preposition* preko; dalje; tamo; **beyond the river** preko reke

biannual dvogodišnji

Bible Biblija

bicycle bicikl

big veliki

bill *check* račun

binoculars dvogled

bird ptica

biro hemijska olovka

birth rođenje; **birth certificate** izvod iz matične knjige rođenih; **birth control** kontracepcija; **to give birth** poroditi se; **to give birth to** roditi

birthday rođendan

bit komadić

bite *verb* ujesti

bitter gorak

black crn

blackboard tabla

black market na crno

blacksmith kovač

bladder bešika

blanket ćebe

bleed krvariti

bless blagosloviti

blind *adjective* slep; **blind people** slepi

blizzard mećava

blocked blokiran; **The toilet is blocked.** Ve-ce/ toalet je blokiran.

blood krv; **blood group** krvna grupa; **blood pressure** krvni pritisak; **blood test** vađenje krvi; **blood transfusion** transfuzija

blow *verb* duvati

blow up *to explode* eksplodirati

blue plav

boar vepar

board *a plane* ukrcati se

boarding pass bording karta

body telo

boil krasta; plih; *verb* vreti

bomb bomba; **bomb disposal** onesposobljavanje neeksplodiranih bombi

bombardment bombardovanje

bone kost

bonnet *of car* hauba

booby trap mina iznenađenja

book knjiga

bookshop knjižara

boot *of car* gepek

boots čizme; **rubber boots** gumene čizme

booth: cashier's booth šalter

border granica; **border crossing** granica; **border guard** graničar

born rođen; **Where were you born?** Gde ste rođeni?; **I was born in New York.** Rođen/rođena sam u Njujorku.

borrow pozajmiti

boss šef

both oba

bottle flaša; **bottle of water** flaša vode

bottle opener otvarač za flaše

bottom *level* dno; donji novo

bowl čanak; **sugar bowl** šećer

box kutija

boxing *sport* boks

boy dečak

boyfriend momak

bra; brassiere brus-halter

bracelet narukvica

braid pletenica

brain mozak

brake *noun* kočnica; *verb* (za)kočiti

branch grana; ogranak

brave hrabar

bread hleb; **to make bread** mesiti hleb

break *for refreshments* pauza; odmor; *verb* napraviti pauzu

break down: pokvariti se; **Our car has broken down** Pokvarila su nam se kola.

breakfast doručak

breast grud; dojka

breathe disati

brew *noun* var; *verb* variti

brick cigla

bride mlada

bridge most

bridegroom mladoženja

briefly ukratko

bright *light* svetlo; *intelligent* pametan

bring doneti

Britain Britanija

British *thing* britanski

Briton Britanac/Britanka

brochure brošura

brother brat; **brothers** braća

brother-in-law *sister's husband* zet; *husband's brother* dever; *wife's brother* šurak; *wife's sister's husband* pašenog

brown braon

bruise *noun* modrica

brush četka

bucket kofa

budget budžet

bug *insect* insekt

build graditi

builder zidar

building zgrada

bull bik

bullet metak

bumper *of car* branik

bureaucracy birokratija

burn *medical* opekotina; *verb* opeći se; goreti

burst rasprsnuti

bury zakopati

bus autobus

bus stop/station autobuska stanica

business *enterprise* preduzeće; *work* posao

businessman poslovan čovek; biznismen

businesswoman poslovna žena

busy zauzet; **The number is busy.** Broj je zauzet.

but a; ali

butcher mesar

butt kraj

butter puter; maslac

butterfly leptir

button dugme

buttonhole rupica za dugme

buy kupiti

buyer kupac

buying kupovanje

by *location* pored; **by bus** autobusom; **by post** poštom; *and see page 21.*

C

cabbage kupus

cabinet *cupboard* ormarić; polica; *political* kabinet

cable kabl; gajtan

cage kavez; **rib cage** grudni koš

cake kolač

calculation računica

calculator digitron

calendar kalendar

calf *animal* tele; *leg* list

call zvati; poziv; **Call the police!** Zovite policiju!

camera fotoaparat; video kamera

camouflage kamuflaža

camp kamp; **Can we camp here?** Možemo li da kampujemo ovde?

campaign kampanja

campus: university campus univerzitetski okrug

can *noun* konzerva; limenka; *verb* **I can...** Mogu...; **Can I eat?** Mogu li da jedem?

can opener otvarač za konzerve

Canada Kanada

Canadian *person* Kanađanin/Kanađanka

canal kanal

cancel otkazati; **The flight is canceled.** Let je otkazan.

cancer rak

candle sveća; **candles** sveće

candlestick svećnjak

candy bonbona

canister metalna kutija; *military* kerteč; granata sa kertečom

cannon top

capital *city* glavni grad; *financial* kapital

car automobil; kola; auto; **car papers** vozačka dozvola; **car park** parking; **car registration** registracija

care briga; nega

careful oprezan; pažljiv

carefully! oprezno! pažljivo!

cargo tovar

carpenter stolar

carpet tepih; *woven* ćilim

carriage prevoz; kola

carrier bag kesa; torba

carrot šargarepa

carry nositi

cart (zaprežna) kola

carton kutija; tetrapak

cartridge šaržer; municija; **cartridge belt** opasač

cashier blagajnik; kasir

cassette kaseta

cast: plaster cast *medical* gips

castle tvrđava

cat mačka

catch uloviti

caterpillar gusenica

catheter katetar

cattle stoka

cauliflower karfiol

cause *noun* uzrok; *political* ideal; pricip; *verb* uzrokovati

caution opreznost

cave pećina

C.D. ce de; disk

C.D. player ce de

ceasefire zatišje

ceiling plafon; tavanica

celebrate slaviti

cell phone mobilni telefon

cellar podrum

cemetery groblje

center centar

century vek

ceramics keramika

certain siguran

certainly sigurno

chain lanac

chair stolica

chalk kreda

change *noun* promena; *money* kusur; *verb* promeniti; **I want to change some dollars.** Želim da promenim dolare.

channel: T.V. channel televizijski kanal

chapter poglavlje

charcoal(s) ugalj; ćumur

charge: What is the charge? Koja je optužba?

charity *general notion* milosrđe; *organization* dobrotvorna organizacija

chase *verb* goniti

chauffeur šofer; vozač

cheap jeftin

cheaper jeftiniji

check *bank* ček; *verb* proveriti; **Check the oil.** Proverite ulje.

check-in čekiranje; predaja prtljaga

cheek obraz

cheese sir

chemical hemijski

chemistry hemija

cherry trešnja; višnja

chess šah

c = hi*ts*   č = *ch*urch   ć = *ty/chy*   d = *dy*   dž = *j*am

chest *box* kutija; sanduk; *of body* grudi

chew žvakati

chewing gum žvakaća guma

chicken pile; *meat* piletina

chickpeas leblebije

chief šef; načelnik

child dete; *boy* dečak; *girl* devojčica

children deca

chimney dimnjak; odžak

chin brada

China Kina

chinaware porcelan

Chinese *person* Kinez/ Kineskinja; *thing* kineski

chocolate čokolada

choke gušiti se; **He/She is choking!** On/ona se guši!

cholera kolera

choose izabrati

chop *verb* seckati

Christian *person* hrišćanin/ hrišćanka

Christianity hrišćanstvo

Christmas Božić

church crkva

cigarette(s) cigareta/e

cinema bioskop

circle krug

citizen državljanin

citizenship državljanstvo

city grad; **city center** centar grada; **city hall** opština grada; **city map** mapa grada

civil: civil rights građanska prava; civil war građanski rat

civilian *noun* građanin; *adjective* građanski

clan klan; pleme

class *academic* razred/ klasa

clean *adjective* čist; **clean sheets** čista posteljina; *verb* čistiti

clear *adjective* jasan; čist; bistar; *verb* čistiti

clerk službenik; **head clerk** upravnik

client stranka

climate klima

climb *verb* penjati se

clinic klinika

cloak ogrtač

clock sat

close (to) *adjective* blizu

close *verb* zatvoriti; **to close a door** zatvoriti vrata

closed zatvoreno

cloth platno

clothes odeća; **clothes shop** prodavnica odeće

cloud oblak

clover detelina

club klub

clutch *of car* kvačilo

coal ugalj

coarse grub

coast obala

coat kaput

cobbler obućar; šuster

cock; cockerel petao

cockroach buba-švaba

code *regulations* pravilnik; *number* šifra; **international dialing code** međunarodni pozivni broj

coffee kafa; **coffee with milk** bela kafa

coin novčić

coins metalni novac

cold *adjective* hladan; *noun* hladnoća; *medical* prehlada; **cold water** hladna voda; **It is cold.** Hladno je.; **I am cold.** Hladno mi je.; **I have a cold.** Imam prehladu.

collar kragna

colleague kolega

collect pokupiti; skupiti

college koledž; fakultet

color boja

comb češalj

come doći; **come in!** Uđite! Napred!

comfortable ugodan; udoban;

This car seat is comfortable. Ovo sedište je udobno.

command komanda

commentary komentar

commission dužnost; komisija; provizija; **What is the commission?** Kolika je provizija?

committee komisija

communications komunikacije

community društvena zajednica

companion drug; pratilac

company *firm* kompanija; firma; preduzeće

compare uporediti

compass kompas

compensation kompenzacija; naknada

competition takmičenje

complain žaliti se

complaint žalba

complete završen; pun; ceo

computer računar; kompjuter; **computer program** kompjuterski program; **computer virus** kompjuterski virus

concert koncert; **concert hall** koncertna dvorana

conciliated pomireni

concussion *medical* potres; udar

condemn osuditi

condition *state* stanje; *term* uslov

condom kondom

conference konferencija

conference room sala za konferencije

confirm: I want to confirm my flight. želim da potvrdim let.

confuse zbuniti

confused zbunjen

connect povezati

connection veza

conquer nadvladati; pokoriti

consider razmotriti; smatrati

constant stalan

constipated: Are you constipated? Imate li zatvor?

constipation zatvor

constitution konstitucija; sastav; ustav

consulate konzulat; predstavništvo

consult konsultovati se; pitati za savet; posavetovati se

consultant konsultant; savetnik

contact veza; kontakt

contact: I want to contact my embassy. Želim da kontaktiram svoju ambasadu.

contact lenses sočiva

contain sadržavati

container *freight* kontejner

contemporary savremen

contest takmičenje; spor

continue nastaviti; **continue!** nastavite!

contract ugovor

control *verb* kontrolisati; nadzirati

conversation razgovor

converse razgovarati

cook *noun* kuvar; *verb* kuvati

cooked kuvan

cooker šporet

cooking pot lonac

cool *adjective* hladan

cooperation saradnja

copper bakar

copy *noun* primerak; kopija; *verb* kopirati; *in school* prepisivati

cork čep; zapušač; *material* pluta

corkscrew otvarač za flaše

corn kukuruz

corner ugao

correct *adjective* tačan; *verb* ispraviti

corridor hodnik

corrupt izopačen; korumpiran

corruption pokvarenost; korupcija

cost *verb* koštati

cot krevetac

cottage cheese seljački sir
cotton wool vata
cough *noun* kašalj; *verb* kasljati
council savet; veće
count brojati
counterfeit falsifikat; **This money is counterfeit.** Ovaj novac je falsifikovan.
country zemlja
countryside priroda
coup d'etat vojni puč
courage hrabrost
court *law* sud
cousin *male* brat; *female* sestra; *distant* rođak
cow krava
crab rak
cradle kolevka
craftsman zanatlija
crane *machine* dizalica
crash *verb* skrhati; slomiti
crayon olovka
crazy lud
cream *ointment* krema
create stvarati
credit kredit
credit card kreditna kartica
cricket *insect* cvrčak; *game* kriket
crime zločin; kriminal
criminal zločinac; kriminalac
crisis kriza
Croat Hrvat/Hrvatica
Croatia Hrvatska
Croatian hrvatski
cross *verb* preći
crossing prolaz
crossroads raskrsnica
crow vrana
cruel okrutan
cry *to weep* plakati
cucumber krastavac
cultivate gajiti; kultivisati
culture kultura
cup šolja
cupboard polica; ormarić

cure *noun* lek; *verb* lečenje
currency novac; novčana jedinica
curtain zavesa
cushion jastučić
custom običaj; *border* carina
cut *verb* seći
cut off: I've been cut off. *on the phone* Izgubio sam vezu.; **The electricity has been cut off.** Nestala je struja.

D

dagger nož
daily dnevno; svakog dana
dairy *noun* mlekara; *adjective* mlečni
dam brana; nasip
damp *noun* vlaga; *adjective* vlažan
dance ples; igra
dancing plesanje; igranje
Dane Danac/ Dankinja
danger opasnost
dangerous opasan
Danish danski
dark *adjective* mračan
darkness *noun* mrak; tama
date *time* datum; **date of arrival** datum dolaska; **date of departure** datum odlaska; **date of birth** datum rođenja; **What's the date today?** Koji je (danas) datum?
daughter kćer; kćerka; *of wife's first husband* pastorka; **daughters** kčeri; kćerke
daughter-in-law snaha; snaja
dawn *noun* zora
day dan; **What day is it (today)?** Koji je danas dan?
dead mrtav
deaf gluv
dear *loved* drag(i)
death smrt
debt dug

h = lo*ch*/*hi*t   j = yet   š = *sh*ip   ž = a*z*ure

decade decenija
deceive prevariti
December decembar
decide odlučiti
decision odluka
declaration deklaracija; objava
decrease *verb* smanjiti
deep dubok
deer jelen
defeat *noun* poraz; *verb* poraziti
defeated poražen
defend odbraniti
degree *grade* stepen; *academic* fakultet; visoka stručna sprema
delay *noun* zakašnjenje
delayed: The plane is delayed. Avion kasni.
democracy demokratija
demolish porušiti
demonstration *political* demonstracije
demonstrators *political* demonstratori
denounce proglasiti; optužiti
dentist zubar
deodorant dezodorans
department odeljenje
department store robna kuća
departure odlazak
departures odlasci
depth dubina
descend silaziti
describe opisati
desert *noun* pustinja
desk radni sto
dessert dezert; slatkiš
destination mesto; cilj
destiny sudbina
destroy uništiti
detergent deterdžent; prašak za pranje rublja
detonate detonirati; prasnuti
detonation detonacija; eksplozija; prasak
development razvoj
devil đavo

dew rosa
diabetes dijabetes; šećerna bolest
diabetic dijabetičar
diagnosis *medical* dijagnoza
dial *verb* birati; **Can I dial direct?** Mogu li da zovem direktno?; **Should I dial this number?** Treba li da biram ovaj broj?
dialect dijalekt
diaper pelene; **I need to change my baby's diaper.** Moram da promenim bebi pelene.
diarrhea proliv
diaspora dijaspora
dictionary rečnik
die umreti
diesel dizel gorivo
diet dijeta
difference razlika
different različit; drugačiji
difficult težak
dig kopati
dining room trpezarija
dinner večera
diplomat diplomata
diplomatic ties diplomatske veze
direct *adjective* direktan; *verb* upravljati
direction *to a place* pravac; *act of direction* upravljanje; **Can you give me directions to...** Pokažite mi put do...
director director; **director's office** direkcija; direktorat
directory adresar
dirty prljav
disability nesposobnost
disabled *adjective* onesposobljen; *noun* invalid(i)
disaster nepogoda
discover otkriti
discuss diskutovati; razmatrati
dicussion diskusija; debata; razmatranje

c = hi*ts*   č = *ch*urch   ć = *ty/chy*   d = *dy*   dž = *j*am

disease bolest
dish jelo
disorderly neuredan; protivzakonit
displaced person raseljeno lice
dispute *noun* spor
distant udaljen
distinction *difference* razlika
district oblast
divide podeliti
division deljenje
divorce *noun* razvod braka
dizzy zbunjen; **I feel dizzy.** Vrti mi se u glavi.
do raditi; **do not...!** nemoj(te)...!
doctor doktor
document dokument
dog pas
doll lutka
dollar dolar
domestic *animal* domaća životinja
donkey magarac
door vrata; **door lock** brava
double *verb* udvostručiti
doubt *noun* sumnja
dough: **to make dough** mesiti testo
dove golubica
down dole
dowry miraz
dozen tuce
drag *verb* vući
dragonfly vilinski konjic
drain *noun* odvod; kanalizacija
draw *an image* crtati
drawer fijoka
drawing *image* crtež
dream *noun* san; *verb* sanjati
dress *noun* haljina; *verb* oblačiti
dressed: **to get dressed** oblačiti se; obući se
dressing *medical* zavoj
dressmaker krojač
drill *verb* bušiti; **to drill a well** kopati bunar
drink *noun* piće; *verb* piti

drinking water voda za piće
drive *verb* voziti
driver vozač
driver's license vozačka dozvola
drug *medical* lek; *narcotic* droga; **drug addict** narkoman
drum *noun* bubanj
drunk: **to be drunk** pijan
dry suv
duck patka
during za vreme; u toku
Dutch *language* holandski
Dutchman Holanđanin
Dutchwoman Holanđanka
duty *obligation* obaveza; *customs* carina
duvet jorgan
dynamo dinamo
dysentery dizenterija

E

each svaki
eagle orao
ear uho; uvo; **ear drum** bubna opna; **ears** uši
early rano; **He is early.** Poranio je.
earn zaraditi
earrings zarada
earth zemlja
earthquake zemljotres
ease *noun* lakoća; *verb* olakšati
east *noun* istok
east(ern) *adjective* istočan
easy lako
Easter Uskrs
eat jesti
economics ekonomija
economist ekonomista
economy *of country* ekonomija
eczema ekcem; lišaj
edible jestiv
editor urednik
education obrazovanje
egg jaje; **boiled egg** kuvano jaje
eggplant plavi patlidžan
eight osam

eighteen osamnaest
eighty osamdeset
either... or ili... ili
elbow lakat
elder brother stariji brat
elect izabrati
election izbor(i)
electric shock električni udar
electricity struja
elephant slon
elevator lift
eleven jedanaest
eloquent rečit
e-mail imejl; električna pošta; **e-mail address** imejl adresa
embassy ambasada
embroidery vez
emergency uzbuna
emergency exit izlaz u nuždi
empty *adjective* prazan; *verb* prazniti
end *noun* kraj; *verb* završiti
enemy neprijatelj
engine motor
engineer inženjer
England Engleska
English *language/thing* engleski
Englishman Englez
Englishwoman Engleskinja
enough dovoljno; dosta
enquiry istraga
enter ući
enterprise preduzeće
entire sav
entrance ulaz
envelope koverat
epidemic *noun* epidemija; zaraza
epilepsy epilepsija
equal jednak
equipment oprema
equivalent jednak; ekvivalentan
eraser gumica za brisanje
escape izbeći; pobeći
especially posebno
essay esej
establish uspostaviti; osnovati

estimate proceniti
eternal večan
etiquette učtivost; bonton
euro *currency* evro
Europe Evropa
European *thing* evropski
European Union Evropska Zajednica; Evropska Unija
evacuate evakuisati
even čak; **even if** čak iako
evening veče; **this evening** večeras
every svaki
everybody svi
everyone svi
everything sve
evidence dokaz
evident jasan; očigledan
ewe ovca
exact tačan; egzaktan
exam ispit
examine *medically* pregledati
example primer; **for example** na primer
excellent odličan
except (for)... osim
excess višak; neumerenost
exchange razmena; **Do you exchange money?** Da li menjate novac?
excuse *noun* izgovor; **excuse me!** Izvinite!
execute *verb* izvršiti; pogubiti
executive izvršni rukovodilac
exercise *noun: activity* vežbanje; fizička aktivnost; *school* vezbanje; **exercise book** sveska za vežbanje
exhaust *of car* auspuh
exhaustion iscrpljenost
exhibition uzložba
exit *noun* izlaz; *verb* izaći
expect očekivati
expel izbaciti
expensive skup
explain objasniti
explanation objašnjenje;

c = hi**ts**   č = **ch**urch   ć = t**y/chy**   đ = **dy**   dž = **j**am

explanations objašnjenja
explode eksplodirati
explosion eksplozija
explosives eksploziv(i)
export *verb* izvoziti; izvesti
exports izvoz
express *fast* ekspres
expression izraz; izražavanje
extra dodatan; poseban
extract *verb* izvući; *noun* izvod; odlomak
extradition izručivanje zločinaca; ekstradicija
eye oko; eyes oči
eyebrow obrva; eyebrows obrve
eyeglasses naočari
eyelashes trepavice
eyesight vid

F

fabric materijal; platno
face *noun* lice; *verb* suočiti se sa
fact činjenica
factory fabrika
faculty *of university* fakultet
fail: to fail an exam pasti ispit
failure neuspeh; poraz
faith vera; veroispovest
falcon soko
fall *autumn* jesen; *noun* pad; *verb* pasti; to fall over pasti
false lažan
family porodica
famine glad
famous poznat; slavan
fan lepeza; *electric* ventilator
fan belt kaiš ventilatora
far daleko
fare karta; What is the fare? Koliko košta karta?
farm farma
farmer poljoprivrednik; zemljoradnik
farming poljoprivreda; zemljoradnja; stočarstvo
fashion moda

fast *quick* brz
fasten pričvrstiti
fat *adjective* debeo; *noun* salo; animal fat mast
father otac; fathers očevi
father-in-law *husband's father* svekar; tast *wife's father*
fatherless bez oca
fax faks; fax machine faks
fear *noun* strah; *verb* strahovati; bojati se
feast gozba
February februar
federation federacija
feed *verb* hraniti
feeding station kantina
feel osećati
felt-tip pen flomaster
female *adjective* ženski; *noun* žena; *animal* ženka
fence ograda
fender *of car* branik
ferret lasica
ferry feribot
fertile plodan
fertilizer (veštačko) đubrivo
festival festival
feud razmirica; krvna osveta
fever groznica
field polje
fifteen petnaest
fifty pedeset
fight *noun* sukob; tuča; bitka; *verb* boriti se
fighting svađa
fighter borac
file *paper* fascikla; *computer* fajl
fill puniti; to fill in a form popuniti formular
film *movie/camera* film; film festival filmski festival
filmmaker filmski reditelj
filter *noun* filter
final *adjective* poslednji; zaključujući; *noun* finale

finance

finance *money* novac; *financial affairs* finansije

find naći

fine *adjective/adverb* fin(o); *of money* kazna

finger prst; **fingers** prsti

fingernail nokti

finish *verb* završiti

fire vatra; *fire as a disaster* požar

firewood drva za potpalu

firm čvrst

first prvi; **first aid** prva pomoć; **first class** prva klasa

fish riba

fishing ribarenje; **fishing net** ribarska mreža

fist šaka

five pet

fix popraviti; namestiti

flash sjaj; blesak; *camera* blic; **flash of lightning** munja

flashlight svetla (na kolima)

flask boca; termos

flat tire izduvana guma; **I have a flat tire.** Ispustila mi je guma.

flea buva

flee bežati

flight *plane* let; *escape* beg

flock stado

flood *noun* poplava

floor *ground* pod; *story* sprat

florist cvećar

flour brašno; **flour mill** mlinara

flow tok

flower cvet

flu grip

fly *noun* mušica; *verb* leteti

fog magla

foggy maglovito

folk *noun* narod

folk dancing narodna igra; folklorna igra

folklore folklor; narodna baština

folk music narodna/folklorna muzika

follow pratiti

food hrana

fool *noun* budala

foot stopalo; *measurement* stopa

football fudbal

footpath staza

for za; **for the sake of** zbog; u korist...

forbid zabraniti

forbidden zabranjen

force sila; snaga

forearm podlaktica

forehead čelo

foreign stran

foreigner stranac

forest šuma

forget zaboraviti

forgive oprostiti

forgotten zaboravljen

fork viljuška

form *official* formular; *shape* oblik

fort utvrđenje

fortnight dve nedelje

forty četrdeset

forward(s) napred

foundation *building* temelj; *organisation* organizacija; fondacija

four četiri

fourteen četrnaest

fourth četvrti

fox lisica

fracture *noun* prelom; *verb* slomiti

fragrance miris

free *liberated* slobodan; **free of charge** besplatan; **free time** slobodno vreme; **Is this seat free?** Je li ovo mesto slobodno?; *verb* osloboditi

freedom sloboda

freeze zamrznuti; smrznuti

freezing smrzavanje

freight *noun* tovar

French francuski

french fries pomfrit

c = hi*ts*   č = *ch*urch   ć = *ty/chy*   d = *dy*   dž = *j*am

Frenchman Francuz
Frenchwoman Francuskinja
frequently često
fresh *food* svež; *cool* hladan
Friday petak
fridge frižider
friend *male* prijatelj; *female* prijateljica
friendship prijateljstvo
frighten uplašiti
frog žaba
from iz
front *adjective* prednji; *noun* lice; prednji deo; **military front** front
frontier granica
frost mraz
frostbite promrzline
fruit voće; **fruit juice** voćni sok
fry *verb* pržiti
fuel gorivo; **fuel dump** skaldište goriva
full pun; **full moon** pun mesec; **to be full** ispunjen
full up: I am full up! Ja sam sit.
funeral sahrana
funny smešan
furniture nameštaj
furrow brazda
future budućnost

G

gain *noun* dobitak; *verb* steći
gala svečanost
gale bura
gall bladder žuč
gallon galon
gamble kockati se
game igra
gandana *leek* praziluk
gangrene gangrena
garage garaža
garden bašta
gardener baštovan
garlic beli luk
garrison garnizon; posada

gas *petrol* benzin; **gas bottle/canister** rezervoar
gasoline benzin
gate kapija
gather skupiti
gazelle gazela
gear *car* brzina
general *adjective* generalan; opšti; *noun* general
generally uglavnom
genitals genitalije
genocide genocid
gentleman gospodin
gently! polako!
geography geografija
geologist geolog
German *person* Nemac/Nemica; *thing/language* nemački
Germany Nemačka
germs bakterije; bacili
get dobiti; **to get in** *to a vehicle* ući (u vozilo); **to get up** ustati
gift poklon
ginger đumbir
girl devojka; **girls** devojke
girlfriend devojka
give dati; **give me...** daj(te) mi...; **to give oneself up** predati se; **to give birth (to)** poroditi se
glacier glečer; lednik
glass *substance* staklo; *drinking* čaša; **glass of water** čaša vode
glasses *spectacles* naočari
gloves rukavice
glue lepak
go ići; **to go over there** preći; **to go out** izaći; **to go to bed** iči u krevet; ići na spavanje; **go!** idi!
goal *football* gol
goat jarac; *kid* jare; *meat* jaretina
God bog
gold zlato
good dobro; **good and evil** dobro i zlo

h = lo*ch/h*it   j = *y*et   š = *sh*ip   ž = a*z*ure

good night!

good night! laku noć!
good-bye! doviđenja!
goose guska
government vlada
grain zrno; seme
gram gram
grammar gramatika
granddaughter unuka
grandfather deda
grandmother baba
grandson unuk
grapefruit grejpfrut
grapes grožđe
grasp *verb* obuhvatiti; shvatiti
grass trava
grasshopper skakavac
grateful zahvalan; **I am grateful.**
  Zahvalan sam.
grave *noun* grob
gravel šljunak
gray siv
great veliki
great-granddaughter praunuka
great-grandfather pradeda
great-grandmother prababa
great-grandson praunuk
great-great-granddaughter
  čukununuka
great-great-grandson čukununuk
Greece Grčka
Greek *noun* Grk/Grkinja; *thing/
  language* grčki
green zelen
greengrocer piljar
grenade granata
grey siv
grief bol
grind *verb* mrviti; mleti
ground zemlja; tlo; pod
group grupa
grow rasti; **to grow up** porasti;
  to grow crops gajiti
guard *noun* stražar; čuvar; *verb*
  stražariti
guerrilla gerila
guest gost

guesthouse gostionica; pansion
guide *noun* vodič; *verb* voditi
guidebook vodič
gum *glue* lepak; guma; **gums**
  desni
gun pistolj; puška
gunman revolveraš
gust izliv; udar
gut crevo; **guts** creva; utroba
gynecologist ginekolog

H

hail *noun* grad
hair kosa
hairbrush četka
haircut: **I want a haircut please.**
  Želim šišanje.
hairdresser frizer
hairdryer fen
half pola; **half year** pola godine;
  polugođe (school)
half-brother polubrat
half-hour pola sata
half-sister polusestra
hammer *noun* čekić
hand *noun* ruka; **to hand over**
  isporučiti
handbag ručna tašna
handful šaka
handicraft ručni rad
handkerchief maramica
handle *noun* ručka
hang okačiti
hangar hangar
hanger *clothes* vešalica; ofinger
happen dogoditi se
happy srećan
hard *difficult* težak; *not soft* tvrd
hardware store gvožđara
hare zec
harmful štetan
harvest žetva
hashish hašiš
hat šešir; kapa; *fur hat* šubara
hate *noun* mržnja; *verb* mrzeti
have imati; **to have to** morati

c = hi**ts**   č = **ch**urch   ć = **ty/chy**   d = **dy**   dž = **j**am

hawk soko; jastreb
hay seno
he on
head glava; *boss* glava; vođa
headache glavobolja
headmaster direktor škole
headquarters štab
headscarf *woman's* marama
heal zaceliti; zarasti; izlečiti
health zdravlje
healthcare zdravstvo
healthy zdrav
hear čuti
heart srce; **heart attack** srčani udar; **heart condition** srčani problem; preoblem sa srcem
heat *noun* vrućina; *verb* zagrejati
heatwave topli talas
heaven nebo
heavy težak
hedgehog jež
heel peta
height visina
helicopter helikopter
hell pakao
hello! zdravo!
help *noun* pomoć; *verb* pomoći; **help!** Upomoć!; **Can you help me?** Možete li mi pomoći?/Molim vas pomozite mi.
hem rub
hen kokoška
hepatitis hepatitis; žutica
her nje; nju; je; njoj; joj; njen; **This is from her.** Ovo je od nje.; **I told her.** Rekao sam njoj./ Rekao sam joj.; **I see her.** Vidim nju./ Vidim je.; **her book** Njena knjiga.
herb trava; začin
herd stado
here ovde
hero heroj
hers njen
herself sebe

hidden skriven
hide sakriti
high visoko; **high blood pressure** visok krvni pritisak
high school srednja škola
highway autoput
hijack napasti iz zasede
hijacker napadač iz zasede
hijacking napad iz zasede
hike *verb* pešačenje
hill brdo
him njega; ga; njemu; mu; njegov; **This is from him.** Ovo je od njega.; **I told him.** Rekao sam njemu./Rekao sam mu.; **I see him.** Vidim njega. / Vidim ga.
himself sebe
Hindi Hindi
Hindu Indus
Hinduism hinduizam
hip kuk
hire iznajmiti
his njegov; **his book** njegova knjiga
historian istoričar
history istorija
hit *verb* udariti
hold držati
hole rupa
holiday praznik; **holidays** odmor; **school holidays** raspust
holy sveti; **holy man** svetac
homeland otadžbina
homeless: homeless person beskućnik
homework domaći zadatak
honey med
honor čast
hood *of car* poklopac
hook *noun* kuka
hope nada
horn rog; *car* sirena
hornet stršljen
horse konj; **horses** konji; **horse racing** konjske trke

h = lo*ch*/hit   j = yet   š = s*hip*   ž = a*z*ure

horseback riding jahanje

hospitable gostoljubiv; gosto-primljiv

hospital bolnica

host domaćin

hostage taoc; **to take hostage** zarobiti

hostel pansion; gostionica

hot vruć; **hot water** vruća voda; **I am hot.** Vruće mi je./ Vrućina mi je.; **It is hot.** Vruće je./Vrućina je.

hotel hotel

hour sat

house kuća

how? kako? koliko?; **how many?** koliko?; **how much?** koliko?; **how much is it?** Koliko košta?; **How much does this cost?** Koliko ovo košta?; **How far?** Koliko daleko?; **How far is the next village?** Koliko daleko je sledeće mesto/ selo?

however ali; međutim

human (being) *noun* ljudsko biće; *adjective* ljudski; čovečiji; **human rights** ljudska prava

humanitarian humanitaran; **humanitarian aid** humanitarna pomoć

humid vlažan

humor humor

humorous smešan

hundred sto

hunger glad

hungry gladan; **I'm hungry.** Gladan sam.

hunt lov

hunting lov

hurry: I'm in a hurry. Žurim.; **hurry up!** Požuri(te)!

hurt *noun* povreda; *verb* povrediti; **It hurts here.** Boli me ovde.; **My back hurts.** Bole me leđa.

husband suprug; muž

hygiene higijena

I

I ja

ice led

ice cream sladoled

icy leden

I.D. identifikacija; lična karta

idea ideja

identification identifikacija

if ako; **if not** ako ne; **if possible** ako je moguće

ill bolestan; loš; **to be ill** biti bolestan; **I am ill.** Bolestan sam.

illegal ilegalan; nezakonit

illiterate nepismen

illness bolest

image lik

imagination mašta

immediately odmah

immigrant imigrant

immigration imigracija; doseljenje

impolite neučtiv

import *verb* uvesti; uvoziti

importance značajnost; važnost

important važan; značajan

impossible nemoguć

improve poboljšati

in u; **in addition to** uz to; pritom; **in front of** ispred; **in the country** u zemlji

included uključen

incomplete nepotpun

indeed zaista

independence nezavisnost

independent nezavisan; **independent state** nezavisna država

index finger kažiprst

India Indija

Indian *thing* indijski

indicator light žmigavac

indigestion loše varenje;

c = hi*ts*   č = *ch*urch   ć = ty/*chy*   d = dy   dž = *j*am

problem(i) sa varenjem
industry industrija
infant dete
infected zaražen
infection infekcija; zaraza
inflammable upaljiv
influenza grip
information informacija; **information office** (služba za) informacije
infuse uliti
injure povrediti
injured povređen
injury povreda
ink mastilo
inner-tube unutrašnji guma
innocent nevin
inquiry ispitivanje; istraživanje; pitanje
insane lud; nerazuman
inscription zapis
insect insekt; **insects** insekti
insecticide insekticid; sredstvo protiv insekata
inside u; unutar
insignificant nevažan
instance: for instance na primer
instead umesto
institute institut
instruction *teaching* instrukcija; podučavanje
instructions *on use* uputstvo
insurance osiguranje; **I have medical insurance.** Imam zdravstveno osiguranje.
insured: My possessions are insured. Imam osiguranje za imovinu.
intelligence inteligencija
intelligent inteligentan; pametan; bistar
intend nameravati
intention namera
interest *noun* interesovanje; korist; *financial* interes; kamata; *verb* zainteresovati; interesovati

interesting zanimljiv; interesantan
interior *adjective* unutrašnji; unutarnji; *noun* unutrašnjost; enterijer; **ministry of the interior** ministarstvo unutrašnjih poslova
internal unutrašni; unutarnji
international međunarodni; **international operator** međunarodna centrala; **international code** pozivni broj za inostranstvo; **international flight** međunarodni let
internet internet
interpret tumačiti
interpreter tumač
intersection presecanje; ukrštanje
interval razmak; interval
interview intervju; razgovor
intestines creva
into u
introduce predstaviti
invade napasti; izvršiti invaziju
invasion napad; invazija
investigate istaživati
investigation istraga
invitation poziv; pozivnica
invite pozvati
Iran Iran
Iranian *person* Iranac/Iranka; *thing* iranski
Ireland Irska
Irish *person* Irac/Irkinja; *thing* irski
iron *for clothes* pegla
Islam islam
Islamic islamski
Israel Izrael
Israeli *person* Izraelac/Izraelka; *thing* izraelski
it to; ovo; ono
Italian *person* Italijan/ Italijanka; *language/thing* italijanski
Italy Italija
itch *noun* svrab

h = lo*ch*/h*it*   j = yet   š = *sh*ip   ž = a*z*ure

item

item primerak; predmet; tačka; stvar; par
its njegov

J

jack *of car* dizalica
jackal šakal
jacket jakna
jam pekmez; džem; **traffic jam** špic; gužva
jelly žele
janitor kućni nadzornik; domar
January januar
Japan Japan
Japanese *person* Japanac/Japanka; *language/thing* japanski
jaw vilica
jazz džez
Jew Jevrejin/Jevrejka
jeweler juvelir; zlatar
jewelry nakit; dragocenosti
Jewish jevrejski
job posao; rad
joiner stolar
joint zglob; mesto spajanja; javni lokal
joke *noun* šala
journalist novinar
Judaism judaizam
judge *noun* sudija
jug bokal
juice: fruit juice voćni sok
July juli
jumper džemper
June juni
junior mlađi; junior
just now upravo sada
justice pravda

K

kebab ćevapi
keep *verb* držati
ketchup kečap; paradajz sos
kettle čajnik; lonče
key ključ

kid *goat* jare
kidnap oteti; kidnapovati
kidnapper kidnaper
kidnapping otmica; kidnapovanje
kidney bubreg; **kidneys** bubrezi
kill ubiti
killer ubica
killing ubistvo; ubijanje
kilogram kilogram
kilometer kilometar
kind *adjective* dobar; ljubazan; dobrodušan; *noun* vrst
king kralj
kiosk kiosk
kiss *verb* poljubiti
kitchen kuhinja
kite zmaj
knead mesiti
knee koleno
kneel klečati
knife nož
knit plesti
knock kucati
know znati; **I know.** Znam.; **I don't know.** Ne znam.; **Do you know him/her?** Da li znate njega/nju?; **Do you know Serbian?** Znate li/ govorite li srpski?
knowledge znanje
known poznat; znan
Koran Kuran

L

laboratory laboratorija
lack *noun* manjak; nedostatak
ladder merdevine
ladle kutlača
lake jezero
lamb jagnje; *meat* jagnjetina
lamp lampa
land *noun* zemlja; *verb (airplane)* prizemljiti se; sleteti
landlord gazda
landslide oburvavanje

language jezik
lantern fenjer; lampa
laptop *computer* laptop
large veliki; krupan
last poslednji; prošli; **last night** sinoć; prošle noći; **last week** prošle nedelje; **last year** prošle godine
late kasno; **I am late.** Kasnim.
laugh smejati se
laughter smeh
laundry *clothing* veš za pranje; *place* vešernica
law zakon; pravilo; **law court** sud; sudnica
lawyer pravnik; advokat
lay (down) položiti
laziness lenjost
lazy lenj
lead *noun: metal* olovo
lead *verb* voditi
leader vodič
leaf list
leak *verb* curiti; procuriti
lean *adjective* mršav; *verb* nagnuti se
leap *verb* skočiti; **leap year** prestupna godina
learn učiti; **to learn by heart** naučiti napamet
leather koža
leave *verb* otiči; napustiti
lecture *noun* predavanje
left *side* levo; **to the left** na levo; s' leve strane
left-handed levoruk
left-wing levica (political)
leg noga
legal zakonit; legalan; **legal profession** pravo; pravna profesija
legend legenda
lemon limun
lend pozajmiti
length dužina
lengthen produžiti
lens (stakleno) sočivo

lentils sočivo
leopard leopard
less manje; **-less** bez-
lesson lekcija; čas
let: Let's go! hajdemo!
letter psimo; *of alphabet* slovo; **letters** *of alphabet* slova
lettuce zelena salata
level *adjective* ravan; *noun* nivo
lever poluga
liberate osloboditi
liberty sloboda
library biblioteka; čitaonica
lice vaške
lick lizati
lie *verb* ležati; *to tell a lie* slagati
lie down leći
life život
lifeless beživotan
lift *elevator* lift; *verb* podići
light *noun* svetlo; svetlost; *electric* svetlo; *torch* baklja (primitive); svetiljka; baterijska lampa; *adjective: bright* svetao; *color* svetla boja; *not heavy* lak; *verb* upaliti; osvetliti; rasvetliti; **to light a fire** upaliti vatru; zapaliti vatru; **Do you have a light?** Imate li upaljač?
lightbulb sijalica
lighter upaljač
lightning munja; bljesak; *bolt* grom
like *preposition* kao; *verb* sviđati se; voleti; **I like...** Sviđa mi se... Volim...; **I don't like...** Ne sviđa mi se... Ne volim...
limbs (of body) udovi (tela)
lime *fruit* (zeleni) limun
limit *noun* granica; prepreka; ograničenje; *verb* ograničiti
line linija; crta
linguist lingvist
linguistics lingvistika
lining *of clothes* postava

lion lav
lip usna
lipstick ruž za usne; karmin
liquid tečnost
liquor alkoholno piće
list *noun* spisak; lista
listen slušati
listener slušalac
liter litar
literature literatura; *fiction* književnost
little *small* mali; *less* manje; **little finger** malić; **little by little** malo po malo
live: live broadcast uživo; **live wire** živa žica
live *verb* živeti; *to dwell* stanovati
liver jetra
livestock živina; čeljad
lizard gušter
load napuniti; natovariti
loaf vekna hleba; hleb
local *adjective* lokalan; **a local shop for local people** lokalna prodavnica za meštane
location mesto; lokacija
lock *noun* brava; *verb* zaključati
locomotive lokomotiva
loft tavan; potkrovlje
loins slabine; međunožje
long dugačak
look gledati; **to look for** tražiti
loot *verb* pljačkati
lorry kamion
lose *to mislay* izgubiti; zaturiti; *to be defeated* izgubiti; **I have lost my key.** Izgubio sam ključ.
lost: I am lost. Izgubio sam se.
lot velika količina; **a lot** mnogo
lottery loto
loud glasan
loudly glasno
louse vaška
love *noun* ljubav; *verb* voleti

low nizak; **low blood pressure** nizak krvni pritisak
lower *verb* spustiti
luck sreća
luggage prtljag
lumps *of earth* grudve zemlje
lunch ručak
lungs pluća

M

machete mač
machine mašina
machine gun mašinka
magazine *printed* magazin; časopis
magnetic magnetni
mail pošta
mailbox poštansko sanduče
main glavni; **main square** glavni trg
maintain održa(va)ti
maize kukuruz
majority većina
make napraviti
make-up *cosmetics* šminka
malaria malarija
male *adjective* muški; *noun* muškarac; *animal* mužjak;
mammal sisar
man čovek
manager upravnik; menadžer
manner *mode* način
manual *book* uputstva
manure đubrivo
many mnogi
map mapa; **map of Belgrade** mapa Beograda
March mart
mare kobila
mark znak; oznaka; trag
market tržište; *green market* pijaca
marriage brak
married: I am married. *said by a man* Oženjen sam.; *said by a woman* Udata sam.
marrow *of bone* koštana srž

c = hi**ts**   č = **ch**urch   ć = t**y/chy**   đ = d**y**   dž = **j**am

marry *see* **married**
marsh močvara
martyr mučenik
mascara maskara
mat podloga; *for cup/glasses* podmetač
match *football* utakmica
matches *for fire* šibice
material materijal; *cloth* materijal; platno
mathematics; maths matematika
matter *subject* materija; predmet; stvar/ **It doesn't matter!** Ne mari!/ Nije važno.
mattress dušek
May maj
maybe možda
me mene; me; meni
meadow livada
meal obrok
mean: What does this mean? šta ovo znači?
meaning značenje
measure *verb* meriti
meat meso
mechanic mehaničar
media mediji; sredstva komunikacije; **mass media** mas mediji
medical *adjective* medicinski; **medical insurance** zdravstveno osiguranje
medication lek; medikament
medicine medicina; lek
meet sresti
meeting susret; sastanak
melon dinja
member član
memory uspomena; pamćenje; memorija
men ljudi
menu jelovnik
mercenary najamnik
message poruka
metal *noun* metal; *adjective* metalan

meter metar; *measurement* merilo; mera
metro metro
mid srednji
midday podne
middle sredina
midnight ponoć
midwife babica
mile milja
military *adjective* vojni; **military service** vojna obaveza
milk mleko; **human milk** majčino mleko; **cow's milk** kravlje mleko; **goat's milk** kozje mleko; **powdered milk** mleko u prahu
mill mlin
millennium milenijum
miller mlinar
millet proso
million milion
millstone žrvanj; vodenični kamen
mind *noun* um; duh
mine *adjective* moj; *mineral* rudnik; *explosive* mina; **antipersonnel mine** protivpešadijska mina; **anti-tank mine** protivoklopna mina; **unexploded mine** ne eksplodirana mina
minefield minsko polje
miner rudar
mineral *noun* mineral; **mineral water** mineralna voda
minister *political* minister; poslanik
ministry ministarstvo
minority manjina
mint menta; nana
minute *noun* minut
miracle čudo
mirror ogledalo
mislead prevariti; obmanuti
miss *verb: not hit* promašiti
Miss gospođica
missile projektil

mission misija
mist magla; izmaglica
mistake greška; **to make a mistake** pogrešiti
mix pomešati
mixture smesa
mobile phone mobilni telefon; mobitel
mode način; oblik
model *sample* uzorak; *person* model
modem modem
modern moderan
modest skroman
mole *on skin* mladež; *animal* krtica
moment momenat
monarch monarh
monarchy monarhija
monastery manastir
Monday ponedeljak
money novac
monkey majmun
month mesec
monthly mesečno
monument spomenik
moon Mesec
more više; **more or less** više manje; **more than that** više od toga
morning jutro; **this morning** jutros
mortgage kredit za kuću
mosque džamija
mosquito komarac; **mosquito net** mreža protiv komaraca
most većina; najviše
mother majka; **mothers** majke
mother-in-law *husband's mother* svekrva; *wife's mother* tašta
motherless bez majke; siroče
motorbike/motorcycle motor; motorcikl
motorway autoput
mount *noun* brdo; *verb* **to mount a horse** uzjahati

mountain planina; **mountain pass** planinski prolaz; **mountain stream** planinska reka
mouse miš
mouth usta
move *verb* pomeriti se
movie film
movie theater bioskop
Mr. gospodin
Mrs. gospođa
much mnogo; **not much** ne baš mnogo; ne previše
mud blato
muffler *of car* prigušivač
mug *noun* vrč
mulberry dud
mule mazga
multiplication množenje
multiply množiti (se)
munitions municija
murder *noun* ubistvo; *verb* ubiti; izvršiti ubistvo
murderer ubica
muscle mišić; **muscles** mišići
museum muzej
music muzika; **music festival** muzički festival
Muslim musliman/ muslimanka
must morati
mustache brk
mutton ovčetina
my moj
myself sebe
mystic *person* mistik

N

nail *of finger/toe* nokat; *metal* ekser
naked go; nag
name ime; **What is your name?** Kako se zovete?/ Kako je vaše ime?; **My name is Fred.** Zovem se Fred./ Moje ime je Fred.
napkin salveta

c = hi*ts*   č = *ch*urch   ć = *ty/chy*   d = *dy*   dž = *j*am

nappy pelena; **I need to change my baby's nappy.** Moram da promenim bebi pelene.

narrow uzak

nation narod

national narodni

nationality nacionalnost

natural prirodan; **natural disaster** prirodna nepogoda; **natural resources** prirodna bogatstva

nature *the natural world* priroda

navel pupak

near blizu

nearby blizu; nedaleko

nearly skoro

necessary neophodan; **it's necessary** neophodno je

necessity potreba; nužda

neck vrat

necklace ogrlica

necktie mašna; kravata

need *noun* potreba; **to need** *verb* trebati; **I need...** Treba mi...

needle igla; **Do you have a needle and thread?** Imate li iglu i konac?

negotiator pregovarač; posrednik

neighbor sused; komšija

neither ... nor niti... niti

nephew *brother's son* bratanac; nećak; *sister's son* sestrić

nerve nerv; živac

net: fishing net mreža za ribolov; **mosquito net** mreža protiv komaraca

never nikad

new nov; **new moon** mlad mesec; **new year** nova godina; **New Year celebration** novogodišnja proslava

New Zealand Novi Zeland

newborn child novorođenče

news vesti; novosti

newspaper novine; **daily newspaper** dnevne novine; **newspaper in English** engleske novine; novine na engleskom jeziku

newsstand kiosk; trafika

next sledeći; **next week** sledeće nedelje

nice prijatan; lep

nickname nadimak

niece *brother's daughter* bratanica; nećaka; *sister's daughter* sestričina

night noć

nightclub noćni klub

nightguard noćni čuvar

nightingale slavuj

nightmare noćna mora

nine devet

nineteen devetnaest

ninety devedeset

no ne; **no entry** zabranjen ulaz; **no problem!** nema problema!; **no smoking** zabranjeno pušenje; **no sugar** bez šećera

nobody niko

noise buka; galama

nomad nomad

none nijedan; niko; ništa

noon podne

normal normalan

normally uglavnom

north *noun* sever

north(ern) *adjective* severan

Northern Ireland Severna Irska

Norway Norveška

nose nos

not ne; **not yet** ne još

note: bank note novčanica

notebook sveska

nothing ništa

nought nula

noun imenica

novel roman

November novembar

now sad; sada

h = lo*ch*/*hi*t   j = yet   š = *sh*ip   ž = a*z*ure

nowhere nigde
number broj
nurse medicinska sestra
nut orah

O

objective objektivan; nepristrasan; objektiv (on photo camera)
observer posmatrač
occasionally povremeno; ponekad
occupation *job* zanimanje
occupy a country okupirati
occupying forces okupacione snage
occur dogoditi se; pasti na pamet
ocean okean
o'clock: It is six o'clock. Šest (je) sati.
October oktobar
of od; **the plays of Shakespeare** Šeksirove drame
office služba; poslovnica; kancelarija; **office worker** službenik
officer *military* oficir
official *adjective* zvaničan; *noun* zvaničnik; zaduženo lice; **officials** zvaničnici
often često
oil *cooking/engine* ulje; **oil pipeline** naftovod; **oil refinery** rafinerija nafte; **oil tanker** tanker; brod za prevoz nafte
oilcan kanta za ulje
ointment krema; mast za rane
old star; **old man** starac; **old woman** starica; **old city** stari grad; **How old are you?** Koliko imate godina?/ Koliko ste stari?; **I am ... years old.** Imam ... godina.
on na; **on foot** peške

once jednom
one jedan
oneself sebe
one-way: one-way street jednosmerna ulica; **one-way ticket** karta u jednom pravcu
onion crni luk
only *alone* jedini; sam; *adverb* samo; jedino
onto *preposition* na
open *adjective* otvoren; *verb* otvoriti
operating theater/room operaciona sala
operation *surgical* (hirurška) operacija
operator operater; tehničar; **telephone operator** centrala
opium opijum
opponent protivnik
opposite suprotan
opposition opozicija; otpor; suprotnost
or ili
orange *fruit* pomorandža; *color* narandžast
orchard voćnjak
order *command* naredba; *arrangement* red; poredak; *to command* narediti; narediti; narediti; narediti; narediti; **to order a meal** naručiti
ordinary običan
organ *of body* organ
origin poreklo; početak
original originalan
orphan siroče
orphanage sirotište
other drugi; drugačiji
ounce unca
our naš
ourselves mi; nas
out van; izvan; napolje
outside spoljašnjost; napolju
oven rerna
over preko; više; završen
overcoat ogrtač; kaput

c = hi*ts*   č = *ch*urch   ć = ty/*chy*   d = dy   dž = *j*am

overcome prevazići; savladati
overtake *by car* preteknuti; preticati
overturn preokrenuti
owl sova
own *adjective* vlastit; sopstven; *verb* posedovati; imati
owner vlasnik; *of building* vlasnik zgrade
ownership *of property* vlasništvo
ox vo
oxygen kiseonik

P

pace korak; tempo
package paket; zavežljaj
packet paket; kutija
packhorse tovarni konj
padlock katanac
page strana; stranica
pain bol
painkiller anelgetik; lek protiv bolova
paint *noun* boja; *verb* bojiti; farbati; *artistically* slikati
painter slikar
painting slika
palace palata
pale bled
palm *of hand* dlan
pamphlet pamflet; brošura
pancreas pancreas; gušterača
pane staklo
pantyhose hula-hopke
paper *substance* hartija; papir; *documents* isprave; *newspaper* novine; *article* članak
parachute padobran
paradise raj
paralyze paralizovati (se)
paralyzed paralizovan
parcel paket
parents roditelji
park *noun* park; *verb* parkirati (se)
parliament parlament; skupština

parrot papagaj
part deo
participate učestvovati
partridge jarebica
party *celebration* proslava; žurka; *political* stranka; partija
pass *I.D.* propusnica; identifikacija; **mountain pass** planianski prolaz; *verb* proći; preći; **to pass an exam** proći; položiti ispit; **to pass time** provesti vreme
passable: Is the road passable? Je li put prohodan?
passenger putnik
passer-by prolaznik
passport pasoš
passport number broj pasoša
past *adjective* prošli; *noun* prošlost; **some years past** pre nekoliko godina; **the past century** prošlog veka
pasta testenine; makaroni
path staza
patient *adjective* strpljiv; **Be patient!** Budi(te) strpljivi!
patient *medical* pacijent
patrol patrola; izvidnica
pay *noun* plata; naknada; *verb* platiti
payment isplata
pay-phone javni telefon
peace mir; **peace talks** mirovni pregovori; **to make peace** sklopiti mir
peacekeeping troops mirovne snage; mirovne trupe
peach(es) breskva; breskve
peacock paun
peak vrh
pear kruška
pearl biser
peas grašak
pebble kamenčić
pedestrian *noun* pešak

pediatrician pedijatar; dečiji lekar
pediatrics pedijatrija
pelvis karlica
pen olovka
pencil grafitna olovka; drvena olovka
penicillin penicilin
penknife perorez
pen-name pseudonim
people ljudi; narod
pepper *vegetable* paprika; *spice* biber
perfect savršen
perform izvesti; (iz)vršiti; (od)igrati
performance izvođenje; vršenje; predstava
perfume parfem; miris
perhaps možda
period *of time* period; doba; rok; *class* čas; *menstrual* menstruacija
permitted dozvoljen
person osoba; lice
petition peticija; molba
petrol benzin; **I have run out of petrol.** Nestalo mi benzina.
pharmacy apoteka
pheasant fazan
phone *noun* telefon; *verb* telefonirati; pozvati; **Please phone me.** Molim vas; telefonirajte mi.
photo fotografija; slika
photocopier fotokopir mašina; fotokopirnica
photocopy *noun* fotokopija; *verb* fotokopirati
photographer fotograf
photography fotografija
physical fizički
physics fizika
physiotherapy fizioterapija
piano klavir
pickax trnokop; sekirica
picnic izlet; piknik
picture slika
piece komad; parče
pig prase
pigeon golub
pilgrim hodočasnik
pilgrimage hodočašće; **to go on pilgrimage** ići u hodočašće
pill pilula; tableta
pillow jastuk
pilot pilot
pin igla
pink roze
pipe cev
pipe *smoking* lula
pistol pištolj; revolver
pitch *football* igralište
place *noun* mesto; *verb* postaviti; **place of birth** mesto rođenja
placenta posteljica
plain *noun* ravnica; poljana
plane avion
plank daska
plant *noun: botanical* biljka; *industrial* postrojenje; *verb* (za)saditi
planting setva
plaster *medical* flaster; *for cuts* hanzaplast; *for broken limbs* gips
plastic plastika
plate tanjir
platform *railway* peron; **platform number** broj perona
play *noun: theater* pozorišni komad; drama; *verb* igrati (se); *a musical instrument* svirati
please! Molim (vas/te)!
pleasure zadovoljstvo
plow *noun* plug; *verb* orati
plug *bath* čep; zapušač; *electric* utikač
plum šljiva
p.m. posle podne
poach *animals/game* krasti
pocket džep

c = hi*ts*   č = *ch*urch   ć = *ty/chy*   đ = *dy*   dž = *j*am

poem pesma
poet pesnik
poetry poezija
point *place* mesto; *tip* šiljak
poison otrov
police policija; milicija
policeman policajac
police station policijska stanica
polite učtiv; ljubazan
political politički
politician političar
politics politika
pomegranate nar
pond ribnjak
pony poni
pool mali ribnjak; **swimming pool** bazen
poor siromašan
population populacija; stanovništvo
pork svinjetina
port *naval* luka
portable T.V. portabilni televizor
portion deo; porcija; obrok
portrait portret
position položaj; mesto; stanje
possess posedovati
possibility mogućnost
possibly možda
post office pošta
postcard razglednica; dopisnica
pot ćup; lonac; **cooking pot** lonac
potatoes krompir
pottery lončarstvo
poultry živina
pound *weight/sterling* funta
pour sipati
poverty siromaštvo; oskudica
powder prah; prašak; *cosmetic* puder
power moć; vlast
praise pohvala
pray moliti (se)
prayer molitva
prefer više voleti; preferirarti

pregnant trudna; **I'm pregnant.** Trudna sam.
preparation priprema; **preparations** pripreme
prepare pripremiti; spremiti
present *adjective: time* sadašnji; *noun: time* sadašnjost; *gift* poklon
president *of country* predsednik; *of organisation* predsednik; rukovodilac
press: the press štampa; **freedom of the press** sloboda štampe; **printing press** štamparija; *verb* pritisnuti
pressure pritisak
pretty lep; zgodan
prevent sprečiti
previously ranije
price cena
pride ponos
priest sveštenik
prime minister premijer
prince princ
principal *adjective* glavni; *noun: school* direktor škole
print *verb* štampati
printer *place* štamparija; *computer* štampač
prison zatvor
prisoner zatvorenik; **to take prisoner** zarobiti; uhapsiti
prisoner-of-war ratni zarobljenik
prize nagrada
probability verovatnoća
probable verovatan; moguć; **It is probable.** Moguće je.
probably verovatno
problem problem
product proizvod
profession zvanje; zanimanje; profesija
professional *person* profesionalac
professor profesor; predavač
program: radio program radio

h = lo*ch*/*hit*   j = yet   š = *sh*ip   ž = a*z*ure

program; emisija; **computer program** kompjuterski program

progress napredak; progres

projector projektor

pronounce izgovoriti

pronunciation izgovor

proof dokaz

proper prav; tačan

prophet prorok

proposal predlog

prosthesis *see* **artifical**

protect zaštititi

protection zaštita

protest *noun* protest; *verb* protestovati; negodovati

proud ponosan

prove dokazati

proverb poslovica

province oblast; provincija

provisions zalihe

public phone javni telefon; govornica

publish objaviti

publisher izdavač

pull vući; **to pull out** izvući

pump *noun* pumpa; **water pump** pumpa za vodu; *verb* pumpati; crpiti; **to pump water** pumpati vodu; crpiti vodu

pumpkin bundeva; tikva

puncture rupa; **I have a puncture.** Imam rupu na gumi./ Pukla mi je guma.

punish kazniti

pupil *school* đak; učenik; *of eye* zenica

puppy štene

purple purpuran; ljubičast

pursue goniti

push gurati

put staviti; **to put down** spustiti; **to put in** uvući; ugurati; **to put on** *clothes* obući se

puzzled zbunjen

Q

quail prepelica

quarrel svađa

quarter četvrtina

quarter *area* četvrt; **quarter of an hour** četvrt sata; petnaest minuta

quarterly četvrtgodišnje; svaka tri meseca; *magazine* tromesečnik

queen kraljica

question pitanje

queue *noun* red

quick brz

quickly brzo

quiet *adjective* miran; tih

quietly mirno; tiho

quilt pokrivač

quit prestati; okanuti se

Quran Kuran

R

rabbit zec

rabies besnilo

radar radar

radiator radijator

radio radio; **radio broadcast** radio emisija; **radio program** radio program/ radio emisija; **radio station** radio stanica

radish rotkvica

raid napad; **air-raid** vazdušni napad

railway železnica

railway station železnička stanica

rain kiša; **rain shower** pljusak; **rain storm** oluja; **It is raining.** Pada kiša.

rainbow duga

raisins suvo grožđe

ram ovan

range niz; opseg

rape *noun* silovanje

rapid brz; rapidan

rapidly brzo; naglo; rapidno

c = hi*ts*   č = *ch*urch   ć = *ty/chy*   d = *dy*   dž = *j*am

rat pacov
rate *speed* brzina
ravine gudura
raw sirov
razor brijač
razor blade žilet
reach *to arrive at* doseći; stići
read čitati
reading čitanje
ready spreman; **I am ready.** Spreman sam.
real stvaran
reality stvarnost
realize ostvariti
reap žeti; brati; imati koristi
reason *cause* razlog; **reason for travel** razlog putovanja
rebel *noun* buntovnik
receipt *proof of purchase* potvrda; račun
receive primiti
recent *adjective* skorašnji
recently skoro; nedavno
reception (desk/area) recepcija
recess *break* prekid; recesija
recreation rekreacija
recognize prepoznati
reconciled pomiren
reconciliation pomirenje
record *noun* zabeleške; gramofonska ploča; *verb* zebeležiti
red crven
Red Cross Crveni Krst
referee sudija
refinery rafinerija
refrigerator frižider
refugee izbeglica; **refugees** izbeglice; **refugee camp** izbeglički centar
regime režim
region područje; sfera
regulation propis; pravilo
reign *noun* vladati
reinforcements pojačanje
relationship odnos; veza; *blood* srodstvo

relative *adjective* relativan; odnosan
relatives *blood* rođaci
relax opustiti se
release pustiti; osloboditi
relief aid pomoć; olakšanje
religion religija; veroispovest
religious: religious sect verska sekta
remain ostati
remaining (pre)ostali
remember setiti se
rent *for oneself* kirija; *to someone* iznajmiti
repair *noun* popravka; *verb* popraviti
repeat ponoviti
replace zameniti
reply *noun* odgovor; *verb* odgovoriti
report *noun: news* izveštaj; *verb* izvestiti; javiti
reporter izveštač; reporter
represent predstavljati
representation reprezentacija; prikaz
representative zastupajući; reprezentativan; tipičan
republic republika
research *noun* istraživanje; *verb* istraživati
reservation *ticket* rezervacija
reserve *verb* rezervisati; **Can I reserve a place/seat?** Mogu li da rezervišem mesto?
reside stanovati
resist odoleti; odupreti se
respect poštovanje
rest *remainder* ostatak; *relaxation* odmor; *verb* odmarati (se)
restaurant restoran; gostionica
result rezultat
retreat *verb* povlačiti se
return *verb* vratiti; **return ticket** povratna karta

reverse *verb* vratiti; **to reverse a car** ići u rikverc

review *noun: newspaper* kritika; osvrt; pregled; revija (kind of newspaper)

revolution prevrat; revolucija

rib(s) rebro; rebra

rib cage grudni koš

rice pirinač; riža

rich bogat

ride *a horse* jahati

riding jahanje

rifle puška

right *correct* pravi; ispravan; *side* desno; **legal right** zakonito pravo; **to the right** na desno; s desne strane; **right hand** desna ruka; **You are right.** U pravu ste/si.; **right now** odmah

rights prava; **civil rights** građanska prava; **human rights** ljudska prava; **women's rights** prava žena

right-wing desnica

ring *noun* prsten; igralište; krug; *verb: bell* zvoniti; *verb: phone someone* telefonirati; pozvati; **I want to ring Emma.** Želim da telefoniram Emi/Želim da pozovem Emu.

riot *noun* nered; buna

ripe zreo

rise *verb: prices etc.* podići; povećati

risk *noun* rizik; opasnost; *verb* rizikovati

river reka; **river bank** rečna obala

road put; **road map** mapa; **road sign** znak

roadblock prepreka na putu

roast *noun* pečenje

rob opljačkati; **I've been robbed!** Opljačkan sam!

robber pljačkaš; razbojnik

robbery pljačka

rock stena

rocket raketa

roll up zaviti; umotati; podviti

roof krov

room soba

rooster petao

root koren

rope konopac

rosary brojanica

rose ruža

rotten truo; pokvaren; loš

rough *coarse* grub

round *adjective* okrugao; približan

roundabout *road* okretnica

route put; ruta

row *argument* svađa

row *line* red

royal kraljevski

rub trljati

rubber *substance* kaučuk; *eraser* gumica za brisanje

rubbish đubre; smeće

rubble ruševine

rude neučtiv; grub

rug *see* **carpet**

rugby ragbi

ruins ruševine

rule *government* vladati; *regulation* pravilo

ruler *instrument* lenjir; *person* vlastodržac

run trčati; **to run out (of)** nestati

Russia Rusija

Russian *person* Rus/ Ruskinja

Russian *language* ruski

rust *noun* rđa

rye raž

S

sack *noun* džak; *verb: dismiss* otpustiti

sacred sveti

sad tužan

safe bezbedan; siguran

safety bezbednost; sigurnost; **safety pin** zihernadla

saffron šafran

c = hi*ts*   č = *ch*urch   ć = ty/*chy*   d = *dy*   dž = *j*am

saint svetac
salad salata
salesman prodavac; trgovac
saleswoman prodavačica; trgovkinja
saliva pljuvačka
salt so
saltless neslan; bez soli
salty slan
same isti
sand pesak
sandals sandale
sandwich sendvič
sanitary towel(s) uložak; ulošci
satchel torba
satellite satelit; **satellite phone** satelitski telefon
satisfactory zadovoljavajući
satisfied zadovoljan
Saturday subota
sauce sos
saucer tacna
sausage kobasica
save *rescue* spasiti; *money* uštedeti
saw *noun* testera
say reći
scarf šal
scatter rasipati; raspršiti
school škola; **school pupil** đak; učenik; **school teacher** učitelj; nastavnik
science nauka
scientific naučni
scientist naučnik
scissors makaze
score *noun: sports* rezultat; *verb: football* dati go; postići go; *verb: sports* pogoditi; **What's the score?** Koji je rezultat?; **Who scored?** *in football* Ko je dao go?
scorpion škorpija
Scot Škotlanđanin/ Škotlanđanka
Scotland Škotska
Scottish škotski
screw *noun* šraf
screwdriver šrafciger

scythe *noun* kosa; *verb* kositi
sea more
search (for) tražiti; **to search a person** pretresati osobu; **to search a house** pretresati kuću
season doba; sezona; godišnje doba
seat stolica; sedište; *in vehicle* sedište; *political* mesto
second *adjective* drugi; *noun* sekunda
secondhand polovan
secret *adjective* tajan; *noun* tajna; **secrets** tajne; **secret police** tajna policija
secretary sekretar *male/* sekretarica *female*
section deo; sloj
security obezbeđenje
see videti
seedling sadnica
seeds seme
seek tražiti
seem izgledati
seize zgrabiti; osvojiti
select izabrati
self sebe; se
sell prodati
send poslati
senior *adjective* stariji; viši
sense *meaning* smisao
sentence *of words* rečenica
separate *adjective* poseban
separate *verb* podeliti; rastaviti
separation razdvajanje
September septembar
septic septičan; otrovan
Serb Srbin/Srpinkja
Serbia Srbija
Serbian srpski
series: **radio series** serija; **T.V. series** televizijska serija
serious ozbiljan; **The situation is serious.** Situacija je ozbiljna.
servant sluga
service služba

h = lo*ch*/*hi*t   j = yet   š = *sh*ip   ž = a*z*ure

session termin; sednica; sesija

set komplet; pribor

seven sedam

seventeen sedamnaest

seventy sedamdeset

several nekoliko

severe jak; strog; opasan; **severe heat** jaka vrućina

sew šiti

sewing machine mašina za šivenje

sex *gender* pol; *act* imati seksualan odnos

shade *noun: from sun* hlad; *protection* zaklon; *shadow* senka; *of color* nijansa

shake tresti

shame *noun* sramota; *verb* sramotiti

shampoo šampon

shape oblik

share *verb* (po)deliti

sharp oštar

sharpen zaoštriti

shave brijanje

shaving cream pena za brijanje

shawl šal; ogrtač

she ona

shear strići; šišati

sheep ovca

sheepdog ovčar

sheet *of cloth* čaršav; *of paper* hartija; tabak hartije

shelf polica

shell *military* granata; *sea* školjka

shelter skrovište

shepherd pastir; ovčar; čoban

shine sijati; *noun* sjaj

ship brod

shirt košulja

shock *medical* šok; potres; slom

shoe *noun* cipela; *verb: a horse* potkivati; **shoes** cipele

shoeshop prodavnica cipela

shoot pucati; **Don't shoot!** Ne pucaj!

shop prodavnica

shopkeeper prodavač

shopping kupovina

shore obala

short kratak

shortage nedostatak; nestašica

shoulder rame; **shoulder blade** lopatica

shout *verb* vikati

shovel lopata

show *noun: fair* izložba; predstava; sajam; **trade show** sajam

shower *bath* tuš; *action* tuširanje; *of rain* pljusak

shrapnel šrapnel

shut zatvoriti

sick bolestan; **I am sick.** Bolestan sam.

sickle srp

side strana; **to the side** sa strane

sidestreet sporedna ulica

siege opsada

sight *eyesight* vid

sign *noun* znak; *verb* označiti

signature potpis

sign language jezik simbola; gestovni jezik

silence tišina

silencer *of car* prigušivač

silent tih; ćutljiv; **to keep silent** ćutati

silk svila; **silk worms** svilena buba

silken svilen

silly luckast

silver srebro

similar sličan

simple jednostavan

since od; **since Monday** od ponedeljka

sing pevati

single jedan; pojedinačan; sam; *not married man* neoženjen; *not married woman* neudata;

single room jednokrevetna soba

sink noun (kitchen sink) sudopera; verb potonuti

sister sestra; sisters sestre

sister-in-law brother's wife snaha; snaja; husband's brother's wife jetrva; husband's sister jetrva; wife's sister svastika

sit sesti

sitting sedenje

situation položaj; situacija

six šest

sixteen šesnaest

sixty šezdeset

size veličina

ski verb skijati

skiing skijanje

skill veština; sposobnost

skilled vešt; umešan

skin koža

skull lobanja

sky nebo

slaughter an animal klati; zaklati

slave rob

sleep verb spavati; to go to sleep ići na spavanje; zaspati

sleeping bag vreća za spavanje

sleeping pill(s) tablete za spavanje

sleepy pospan

sleet susnežica

sleeve rukav

slip verb okliznuti se

slippery klizav

slope padina; nagib

slow spor

slowly! polako!

small mali

smell noun miris

smoke noun dim; verb pušiti (se)

smoker pušač

smoking pušenje

smooth gladak; nežan

smuggler švercer

snack zalogaj; meze; grickalice

snail puž

snake zmija

snakebite ugriz zmije; ujed zmije

sneeze noun kijanje; verb kijati

snore verb hrkati

snow sneg; snowflakes pahulje; It is snowing. Pada sneg.

so tako; toliko; dakle; so much/many toliko

soap sapun

soccer fudbal; soccer match fudbalska utakmica

social društven

society društvo

socks čarape

soft mek

soil tlo; zemlja

soldier vojnik

sole đon; taban; list (fish)

solve rešiti

some neki; nekoliko

somebody neko

somehow nekako

someone neko

something nešto

sometimes ponekad

somewhere negde

son sin; sons sinovi

son-in-law zet

song pesma; love song ljubavna pesma

soon uskoro

sore bolan; osetljiv; I have a sore throat. Boli me grlo.

sorrow tuga

sorry! izvinite!/ žao mi je!

sort noun vrsta

soul duša

sound zvuk

soup supa

sour kiseo

source izvor

south noun jug

south(ern) adjective južni

sow verb sejati

h = loch/hit   j = yet   š = ship   ž = azure

space

space prostor
spade lopata
span raspon
Spaniard Španac/Španjolka
Spanish *language/thing* španski
spanner *wrench* izvijač; natezač
spare preostao; suvišan; **spare tire** rezervna guma
sparrow vrabac
sparrowhawk kobac
speak govoriti; **Do you speak English?** Govorite li engleski?; **I speak English.** Govorim engleski.
speaker govornik; spiker; *on radio, etc.* voditelj; spiker; *of parliament* govornik; predsednik
specialist stručnjak; specijalista
spectacles naočari
speed brzina
spell: **How do you spell that?** Kako se to piše?
spend: **to spend money** trošiti novac; **to spend time** provesti vreme
spice začin
spicy *hot* ljut
spider pauk
spill prosuti
spin okretati
spinach spanać
spinal column kičmeni stub
spine kičma
spit *verb* pljunuti
splint *medical* udlaga
split *verb* deliti; rascepiti
spoil pokvariti
sponge sunđer
spoon kašika
sports sportovi
sportsman sportista
spread *noun* pokrivač; *verb* širiti
spring *metal* feder; *of water* izvor; *season* proleće
sprout *noun* klica; mladica
spy *noun* špijun

square kvadrat; skver; **town square** skver; trg
squeeze stisnuti; cediti
squirrel veverica
stadium stadion
staff osoblje
stag jelen
stage *theater* pozornica; scena
stairs stepenice
stale bajat (bread); bljutav (taste)
stallion ždrebac
stamp *postal* poštanska marka; markica; *official* pečat; žig; **to stamp a document** overiti; udariti pečat
stand *verb* stajati
star zvezda; **stars** zvezde
start *verb* početi
state *noun: condition* stanje; *federal* država; *verb* navesti; ustanoviti
station stanica
stationery shop knjižara; prodavnica pisaćeg pribora
stationery pisaći pribor
statue kip; statua
stay ostati
steak komad mesa; biftek
steal krasti
steam *food* kuvati na pari
steel *noun* čelik; *adjective* čeličan
steering wheel volan
stem deblo; stabljika
stepdaughter pastorka
stepfather očuh
stepmother maćeha
stepson posinak
sterling pravi; punovredan; sjajan
stethoscope stetoskop
stick *noun* prut; štap; *verb* postaviti; zalepiti; zaglaviti; **walking stick** štap
still *yet* još
sting *verb* ubosti
stink *verb* smrdeti

c = hi*ts*   č = *ch*urch   ć = t*y*/*chy*   d = *dy*   dž = *j*am

stir mešati

store *shop* prodavnica

stitch *noun* šav; šiti; *verb* ušivati

stitches *surgical* ušivanje; kopče

stomach stomak

stomachache bol u stomaku

stone kamen

stool stolica

stop zastoj; prestanak; tačka; **stop!** stani(te)! stop!; **don't stop!** nemojte da stajete! nastavite!

store *shop* prodavnica; *for storage* skladište

storm oluja

story *tale* priča; bajka; *news* reportaža; *floor* sprat

stove šporet; peć; **heating stove** peć

straight prav; pravo

strange čudan

stranger stranac

straw slama

strawberry jagoda

stream potok; **mountain stream** brzak

street ulica

strength snaga

stretcher *hospital* nosila

strike *noun: from work* štrajk; obustava rada; *verb: hit* udariti; *from work* štrajkovati

string žica

strong jak

structure sastav; struktura; građevina

struggle borba; napor

stuck: Our car is stuck. Zaglavila su nam se kola.

student *university* student

study *noun* istraživanje; studija; *verb* učenje; studiranje; *academic* studiranje; istraživanje

subject predmet

submachine gun mitraljez

submit predati

subtract oduzeti

subtraction oduzimanje

suburb predgrađe

success uspeh

such takav

suck sisati

suddenly ođednom; iznenada

sufficient dovoljan

sugar šećer

suit odelo

suitable odgovarajući

suitcase kofer

sum suma

summer leto

summit vrh

sun sunce

sunblock krema za sunčanje

sunburn (sunčana) opekotina

Sunday nedelja

sunglasses naočari za sunce

sunny: It is sunny. Sunčano je.

sunrise izlazak sunca

sunset zalazak sunca

supermarket samoposluga; supermarket

supper večera

supplies zalihe

supply *verb* nabaviti; obezbediti

sure *adjective* siguran; *adverb* sigurno; svakako

surgeon hirurg

surgery *subject* hirurgija; *operation* (hirurška) operacija

surname *family name* prezime

surprised iznenađen

surprising: to be surprising iznenađujuć

surrender *verb* predati se

surround okružiti

survey *noun* pregled; *verb* pregledati

surveyor nadzornik

suspicion sumnja

swallow *bird* lasta; *verb* gutati

swamp močvara

swear *to curse* psovati; **to swear**

an oath zakleti se

sweat *noun* znoj

sweater džemper

sweep *verb* pomesti

sweeper čistač

sweet *adjective* sladak; *noun* slatkiš

swell oticati

swelling otok

swim plivati

swimming plivanje; **swimming pool** bazen

swimsuit kupaći kostim

switch *noun: electric* prekidač; *verb* **to switch off** isključiti; **to switch on** uključiti

symbol simbol

symptom *medical* simptom

synagogue sinagoga

syntax sintaksa

syringe špric

syrup sirup

system sistem

T

table sto

tablecloth stoljnjak

tablet tableta

tactic taktika

tailor krojač

take uzeti; **to take away** odneti; **to take off** *something* skinuti; **to take out** izneti; **to take shelter** sakriti se; zakloniti se; **What time does the plane take off?** Kada poleće avion?

talk *verb* govoriti; razgovarati

tall visok

tame pitom

tank *petrol* rezervoar; *military* tenk

tanker brod za prevoz nafte

tap česma

tape traka; *cassette* kaseta; traka

tape recorder kasetofon

taste *noun* ukus; *verb* probati

tasteless bezukusan

tasty ukusan

tax *noun* porez; *verb* oporezovati

tax-free neoporeziv

taxi taksi

tea čaj; **black tea** crni čaj; **green tea** biljni čaj; zeleni čaj; **tea with milk** čaj s mlekom; **tea house** čajdžinica

teach učiti; predavati

teacher učitelj; nastavnik; profesor; *primary school* učitelj

team ekipa

teapot čajnik

tear *noun* suza; rupa

tear *verb* cepati

teaspoon kašičica

technical tehnički

technique tehnika

teenager *boy* mladić; tinejdžer; *girl* devojka; tinejdžerka

teeth zubi

telecommunications telekomunikacije

telegram telegram

telephone *noun* telefon; **telephone operator** centrala; *verb* telefonirati; zvati; pozvati

telescope teleskop

television televizija

telex teleks

tell reći

temperature temperatura; **The temperature in summer is high.** Temperature su visoke leti.; **The temperature in winter is low.** Temperature su niske zimi.; **I have a temperature.** Imam temperaturu.

temple *religious* hram

ten deset

tenant (pod)stanar

tend: to tend to the sick brinuti se o bolesnima

tender *sore* ranjav
tennis tenis
tent šator
tenth deseti
termite termit
terrible strašan
territory područje; teritorija
test *noun* test; ispitivanje; *academic* test; ispit; **blood test** vađenje krvi; *verb* ispitivati; testirati; *academic* testirati; ispitivati
testify svedočiti
text tekst
than nego; od; **This book is better than that one.** Ova knjiga je bolja od te./ Ova knjiga je bolja nego ta.
thank *verb* zahvaliti (se); **thank you!** hvala!
thanks! hvala!
that to; taj; *conjunction* da
theater pozorište; teatar
theft krađa
their njihov
theirs njihov
them njih; njima
themselves njih
then onda
theoretical teoretski
theory teorija
there tamo; **there is/are ...** ima...
therefore dakle
thermometer termometar; toplomer
these ovi
they oni
thick *wide* debeo; **thick cloth** debela tkanina; debelo platno; **thick forest** gusta šuma; **thick soup** gusta supa
thief lopov; kradljivac; **thieves** lopovi
thigh butina
thimble naprstak
thin tanak

thing stvar
think misliti; **I think that...** Mislim da...
third treći
thirst žeđ
thirsty žedan; **I'm thirsty.** žedan sam.
thirteen trinaest
thirty trideset
this ovaj; **this (very)** (baš) ovaj; **this morning** jutros; **this afternoon** danas posle podne; **this week** ove nedelje; **this much** ovoliko
thorax trup
thorn trn
those oni
thought misao
thoughtless nepromišljen
thousand hiljadu
thread vlakno; konac
three tri
throat grlo
thrombosis tromboza
throne tron; presto
through kroz; *by means of* kroz; preko
throw baciti; **to throw out** izbaciti
thumb palac
thunder grom
thunderstorm oluja
Thursday četvrtak
tibia cevanica
ticket karta
ticket office prodaja karata; blagajna; *cinema/stadium* biletarnica
tie *necktie* mašna; kravata; *verb* vezati
tight čvrst
tights unihop čarape
time vreme; **at the same time** u isto vreme; **for a long time** dugo vreme; **on time** na vreme; **I don't have time.** Nemam vremena.; **What**

timetable

time is it? Kolko ima sati?; **Has the bus arrived on time?** Je li autobus stigao na vreme?

timetable raspored; **travel timetable** red vožnje

tire *noun* guma; *verb* umoriti (se)

tired umoran; **to get tired** umoriti se

tissue tkivo; *paper tissues* papirnate maramice

to u; na; prema; **I gave it to her.** Dao sam njoj.; **This is superior to that.** Ovo je bolje od toga.; **We are going to Belgrade.** Idemo u Beograd.; **We are going to the seaside.** Idemo na more.

toast *bread* tost; dvopek

tobacco duvan

today danas

toe prst na nozi

together zajedno

toilet(s) toalet; **toilet paper** toalet papir

tomato paradajz

tomb grobnica

tomorrow sutra; **the day after tomorrow** preksutra

ton/tonne tona

tongue jezik

tonight večeras

too *also* takođe; *very* previše; **too little** premalo; **too many** previše; **too much** previše

tools alat

tooth zub; **teeth** zubi

toothache zubobolja

toothbrush četkica za zube

toothpaste pasta za zube

toothpick čačkalica

top vrh

torrent tok; pljusak

torture *noun* mučenje; tortura; *verb* mučiti

tough *meat* žilavo meso; **This meat is tough.** Ovo meso je žilavo.

tourism turizam

tourist turista; **tourists** turisti; **tourist office** turistička agencija

tow *verb* vući; **tow rope** konopac za vučenje; **Can you tow us?** Možete li da nas povučete?

towel peškir

tower toranj; kula

town grad; **town center** centar grada; **town hall** opština; **town square** gradski trg

tracer bullet trasirno zrno

trachea dušnik

track trag; kolosek; putanja

tractor traktor

trade union radničko udruženje

trader trgovac

tradition tradicija

traditional tradicionalan

traffic *noun* saobraćaj; promet; **traffic lights** semafor; **traffic police** saobraćajna policija

train *noun* voz; **train station** železnička stanica

tranquilizer lek za umirenje

transfer flights presedati

transformer transformator

transfusion: blood transfusion transfuzija krvi

translate prevesti

translation prevod

translator prevodilac; tumač

transmit predavati; prenositi

transmitter predajnik

transport *noun* transport; prevoz; *verb* prevoziti

trap *noun* zamka; klopka

trash smeće; gluposti

trauma trauma

travel *noun* putovanje; *verb* putovati

travel agency putna agencija

traveler putnik; **travelers** putnici

c = hi**ts**   č = **ch**urch   ć = **ty/chy**   d = **dy**   dž = **j**am

traveler's checks putni čekovi
tray poslužavnik
treacherous varljiv; izdajnički
treasury *ministry* ministarstvo finansija
treaty pregovaranje; ugovor
tree drvo; **trees** drveće
trench šanac
trial *legal* suđenje; proces; *test* ispit
troops trupe
trouble *inconvenience* neprilika; nevolja; *problems* nevolja; briga; problem; **What's the trouble?** U čemu je problem?
trousers pantalone
truce primirje
truck kamion
true istinit
trunk *box* sanduk; *of car* prtljažnik; *of tree* deblo
truth istina
try pokušati
tube podzemni voz
tuberculosis tuberkuloza
Tuesday utorak
tunnel tunel
Turk Turčin/Turkinja
turkey ćurka
turn *noun* okret; preokret; *verb* okrenuti; skrenuti; **turn left!** skreni(te) levo; **turn right!** skreni(te) desno
turnip bela rotkva
twelve dvanaest
twenty dvadeset
twice dvaput
twins blizanci
twist okretati; zavrtati
twisted uvrnut
two dva
type *noun* tip; vrsta; *verb* kucati na mašini
typewriter pisaća mašina
tyre *noun* guma

U

ulcer čir; **stomach ulcer** čir na želudcu
umbilical cord pupčana vrpca
umbrella kišobran
uncle *father's brother* stric; *mother's brother* ujak
uncomfortable neugodan; neudoban
uncooked nekuvan
under *adverb* dole; ispod; *preposition* pod; ispod; **under the table** ispod stola
underground *adjective* podzemni; tajni; *subway* podzemna železnica
understand razumeti; **Do you understand?** Da li razumete/razumeš?; **I understand.** Razumem.; **I don't understand.** Ne razumem.
underwear donji veš
undo povratiti; poništiti; razvezati
undress: to get undressed svući se
unemployed nezaposlen
unemployment nezaposlenost
unexploded mine ne eksplodirana mina
unfortunate nesrećan
unfortunately nažalost
unfriendly neljubazan; neprijateljski raspoložen
unhappy nesrećan
uniform uniforma
uninformed uniformisan
union savez; udruženje
trade union radničko udruženje
unique jedinstven
unit *military* jedinica
United Nations Ujedinjene Nacije
United States of America Sjedinjene Američke Države (SAD)
university univerzitet

unknown nepoznat
unless osim; izuzev; ako ne
unsuccessful bezuspešan
until do
unwise nepromišljen; nepametan
up gore
upright uspravan
urgently hitno
urine urin
us mi; nas; nama
U.S.A. SAD
use *noun* korist; *verb* koristiti
useful koristan; zgodan
usefulness korisnost; pogodnost
usual uobičajen
usually obično
uterus uterus

V

vacation odmor
vaccinate vakcinisati; pelcovati; **I have been vaccinated.** Vakcinisan(a) sam.
vaccination vakcina
valley dolina
value *verb* ceniti
veal teletina
vegetables *freshly picked* sveže povrće; *on the plate* garnir; garnirano povrće; **vegetable shop** piljara; piljarnica; **vegetable soup** supa od povrća
vegetarian vegetarijanski; **I am a vegetarian.** Ja sam vegetarijanac.
vein vena; žila
venereal disease polna bolest; venerična bolest
veranda veranda; terasa
verb glagol
vertebra pršljen
very vrlo
veto *noun* veto; zabrana; *verb* zabraniti

vice-president *of country* podpredsednik
victim žrtva; **victims** žrtve; **victims of an earthquake** žrtve zemljotresa
victory pobeda
video cassette video; video kaseta
video player video
view *noun* pogled
village selo
villager seljak
vine loza; vinova loza
vinegar sirće
violence nasilje
viper guja; zmija
virus virus
visa viza
visit *verb* posetiti
visitor posetilac
vitamins vitamini
voice glas
volume *size* obim; zapremina; *book* knjiga
vomit *verb* povraćati; **I have been vomiting.** Povraćao/povraćala sam.
vote *noun* glas; *verb* glasati; **to cast a vote** glasati
voting glasanje
voter glasač
vulture kraguj; lešinar; strvinar

W

wage war voditi rat
waist struk
waistband pojas
waistcoat prsluk
wait čekati; **wait a moment!** čekaj(te)!; sačekaj(te) momenat!
waiter konobar
waitress konobarica
waiting čekanje
wake up probuditi se; **Please wake me up at ...** Molim vas probudite me u...

walk *verb* šetati
walking stick štap
wall zid
wallet novčanik
want želeti; **What do you want?** šta želite/ želiš?; **I want ...** želim...; **I don't want ...** Ne želim...
war rat
warm topao
wash prati
washbowl lavor
washed opran
washing powder deterdžent
wasp osa; osica
watch *clock* sat; **to watch** gledati
water voda; **Is there drinking water?** Ima li vode za piće?
water bottle flaša za vodu; boca za vodu
waterfall vodopad
watermelon lubenica
watermill vodenica
way put; *manner* način; **way of life** životni stil
we mi
weak slab
weapon oružje
wear nositi
weasel lasica
weather vreme
weave *verb* tkati;
wedding venčanje
Wednesday sreda
week nedelja
weekend vikend
weekly nedeljno; svake nedelje
weep plakati
weight težina
welcome! dobrodošli!
well *adjective/adverb* dobar/dobro; *noun: of water* izvor
well-known poznat
west *noun* zapad
west(ern) zapadni
wet vlažan; mokar

what? šta?; **what's that?** šta je to?; **what kind?** koje vrste?
whatever bilo šta; šta god; **Take whatever you want.** Uzmite šta god želite.
wheat pšenica
wheel točak
wheelchair invalidska kolica
when? kad; kada
where gde; **where is?** gde je?; **where are?** gde su?; **where from?** odakle?
whether da li; bilo da
which ko; što; koji; **which (one)?** koji
while dok
whistle *noun* žviždati
white beo; belo
whitish beličast
who? ko
whole ceo
why? zašto
wide širok
widow udovica
widower udovac
wife žena
wild *animal* divlja životinja
wild goose divlja guska
will *willpower* volja; *legal* testament
win pobediti; **Who won?** Ko je pobedio?
wind *noun* vetar
wind *verb* zavijati; navijati; **to wind thread** namotavati konac
window prozor
window pane staklo
windpipe dušnik
windshield/windscreen *car* šofer-šajbna
windy vetrovit
wine vino
winter zima
wire žica
wisdom mudrost; **wisdom tooth** umnjak

h = lo*ch*/*h*it   j = *y*et   š = *sh*ip   ž = a*z*ure

wise mudar
wish *verb* želeti
with sa; **I went with him.**
  Otišao/otišla sam sa njim.; **I**
  wrote with this pen. Pisao
  sam ovom olovkom.
without bez; **without work** bez
  posla
witness svedok
wolf vuk
woman žena
womb materica
women žene
wood *substance* drvo; *forest*
  šuma
wool vuna
woolen vunen
word reč
work *noun* rad; *verb* raditi; **I**
  work in a bank. Radim u
  banci.; **The phone doesn't**
  work. Telefon ne radi.
worker radnik
world svet
worms crvi; *medical* gliste
worried zabrinut; **to be worried**
  biti zabrinut; brinuti
worse gore; **I feel worse.**
  Osećam se gore.
worth: to be worth vredeti
wound *noun* rana; *verb* raniti
wrap zamotati
wrench *tool* odvijač
wrestling rvanje
wrist zglob
wristwatch sat
write pisati
writer pisac

writing pisanje
wrong pogrešno

X

X-rays rendgen

Y

yard *courtyard* dvorište; *garden*
  bašta; zemljište; *distance*
  jarda
year godina; **this year** ove
  godine
yearly godišnje; svake godine
yellow žut
yes da
yesterday juče; **the day before**
  yesterday prekjuče
yesterday's jučerašnji
yet još
yogurt jogurt; kiselo mleko
you *singular* ti; *plural* vi
young mlad; **young person**
  mldić/devojka; **young girl**
  devojka; **youngest child**
  najmlađe dete
your *formal singular* vaš;
  informal singular tvoj
yours *formal plural* vaši;
  informal plural tvoji
yourself tebe; tebi; tobom
yourselves vas; vama

Z

zero nula
zipper rajsferšlus; patent
zoo zoološki vrt

SERBIAN
Phrasebook

1. ETIQUETTE

> **HELLO!** — There are several ways to say "hello!" in Serbian, depending to the level of formality:
> **Dobar dan!** *formal*
> **Zdravo!** or **Ćao!** *informal*
> As in English, just say the same back in reply.
> **GOODBYE!** — There are also several ways to say "goodbye!":
> **Doviđenja!** *formal*
> **Zdravo!** or **Ćao!** *informal*
> As with "hello!", just say the same back in reply.

How are you?	**Kako ste?**
(I'm) fine!	**Dobro (sam)!**
See you tomorrow!	**Vidimo se sutra!**
Response:	**Vidimo se (sutra)!**
Welcome!	**Dobrodošli!**
Response:	**(Hvala) Bolje vas našli!**
Please sit down!	**Izvolite, sedite!**
Help yourself!	**Poslužite se!**
Here you are!	**Izvolite!**
congratulations!	**čestitam!**
excuse me!	**izvinite!**
sorry!	**izvinite!** *or* **oprostite!**
	or **žao mi je!**
yes	**da**
no	**ne**
please	**molim**
thank you	**hvala**
you're welcome!	**molim!** *or*
	nema na čemu!

2. QUICK REFERENCE

I	**ja**
you *singular*	**ti**
you *formal/plural*	**vi**
he/she/it	**on/ona/ono**
we	**mi**
they	**oni/one/ona**
this	**ovaj (ova/ovo)**
that	**taj (ta/to);**
	onaj (ona/ono)
these	**ovi (ove/ova)**
those	**ti (te/ta);**
	oni (one/ona)
here	**ovde**
there	**onde**
where?	**gde?**
who?	**ko?**
what?	**šta?**
when?	**kada?**
which?	**koji (koja/koje)?**
how?	**kako?**
why?	**zašto?**
how much?	**koliko?**
how many?	**koliko?**
what's that?	**šta je to?**
is/are there . . . ?	**ima li...?**
where is . . . ?	**gde je...?**
where are . . . ?	**gde su...?**
here is . . .	**ovde je...**
here are . . .	**ovde su...**

h = lo*ch*/*h*it   j = *y*et   š = *sh*ip   ž = a*z*ure

what must I do?	**šta treba da uradim?**
what do you want?	**šta zelite?**
very	**vrlo**
and	**i**
or	**ili**
but	**ali**
I like . . .	**Sviđa mi se...**
I don't like . . .	**Ne sviđa mi se...**
I want . . . *something*	**Želim... *or* Hoću...**
I want to . . .	**Želim da...**
	***or* Hoću da...**
I don't want . . . *something*	**Ne želim... *or* Neću...**
I don't want to . . .	**Ne želim da...**
	***or* Neću da...**
I know.	**Znam.**
I don't know.	**Ne znam.**
Do you understand? *formal*	**Razumete?**
informal	**Razumeš?**
I understand.	**Razumem.**
I don't understand.	**Ne razumem.**
I am grateful. *m*	**Zahvalan sam vam.**
f	**Zahvalana sam vam.**
	***or:* Hvala vam.**
	***or:* Puno vam hvala.**
It's important.	**Važno je.**
It doesn't matter.	**Nije važno.**
No problem!	**Nema problema.**
more or less	**više ili manje**
Is everything OK?	**Je li sve u redu?**
My condolences. *if some-one has died*	**(Primite moje) saučešće.**

Danger!		**Opasnost!**
Could you repeat that?		**Molim vas, ponovite šta ste rekli?**
How do you spell that?		**Kako se to piše?**

I am hot.		**Vrućina mi je.**
I am right.		**Ja sam u pravu.**
I am sleepy.		**Spava mi se.**
I am hungry.	*m*	**Gladan sam.**
	f	**Gladna sam.**
I am thirsty.	*m*	**Žedan sam.**
	f	**Žedna sam.**
I am angry.	*m*	**Ljut sam.**
	f	**Ljuta sam.**
I am happy.	*m*	**Srećan sam.**
	f	**Srećna sam.**
I am sad.	*m*	**Tužan sam.**
	f	**Tužna sam.**
I am tired.	*m*	**Umoran sam.**
	f	**Umorna sam.**
I am well.		**Dobro sam.**
I am cold.		**Hladno mi je.**

—Colors

black	**crn (-a/-o)**
blue	**plav (-a/-o)**
brown	**braon; smeđ (-a/-o)**
grey	**siv (-a/-o)**
green	**zelen (-a/-o)**
pink	**roze**
red	**crven (-a/-o)**
white	**beo (bela/belo)**
yellow	**žut (-a/-o)**

3. INTRODUCTIONS

What is your name? *formal*	**Kako se zovete?**
informal	**Kako se zoveš?**
My name is . . .	**Zovem se...** *or*
	Moje ime je...
May I introduce you to . . .	**(Dozvolite mi) da vas**
	upoznam sa...
This is . . .	**Ovo je...**
my friend	**moj prijatelj** *m;*
	moja prijateljica *f*
my traveling companion	**moj saputnik** *m;*
	moja saputnica *f*
my colleague	**moj kolega** *m;*
	moja koleginica *f*
my relative	**moj rođak** *m;*
	moja rođaka *f*

Forms of address
"Mr." is **Gospodine** and "Mrs." is **Gospođo**, used both in much the same way as in English. When you don't know a person's name, you can use these forms to mean "Sir" and "Madame". Use **Gospođice** for "Miss". Use the vocatives **Profesore** for a professor or teacher, and **Doktore** for a doctor.

—Nationality

Serbia	**Srbija**
Serbian	**Srbin** *m/***Srpkinja** *f*
Where are you from?	**Odakle ste?**
I am from . . .	**Ja sam iz . . .**
America	**Amerike***
Australia	**Australije**

*Note that **-e/-a** are genitive ending for all these countries. Where there's an **-e**, replace it with **-a** for the nominative form, e.g. **Amerika**; or, where there's an **-a**, remove it entirely, e.g. **Japana** becomes **Japan**.

c = hi**ts**   č = **ch**urch   ć = ty/**chy**   đ = d**y**   dž = **j**am

Britain	**Britanije**
Canada	**Kanade**
China	**Kine**
England	**Engleske**
Europe	**Evrope**
Germany	**Nemačke**
Greece	**Grčke**
India	**Indije**
Iran	**Irana**
Ireland	**Irske**
Italy	**Italije**
Japan	**Japana**
the Netherlands	**Holandije**
New Zealand	**Novog Zelanda**
Northern Ireland	**Severne Irske**
Pakistan	**Pakistana**
Russia	**Rusije**
Scotland	**Škotske**
Turkey	**Turske**
the USA	**Sjedinjenih američkih država**
Wales	**Velsa**

I am . . .	**Ja sam...**
American	**Amerikanac** *m*/ **Amerikanka** *f*
Arab	**Arapin** *m*/**Arapinka** *f*
Australian	**Australijanac/ Australijanka**
British	**Britanac/Britanka**
Canadian	**Kanađanin/ Kanađanka**
Chinese	**Kinez/Kineskinja**
Dutch	**Holanđanin/ Holanđanka**
English	**Englez/Engleskinja**
German	**Nemac/Nemica**

Greek	**Grk/Grkinja**
Indian	**Indijac/Indijka**
Irish	**Irac/Irkinja**
Israeli	**Izraelac/Izraelka**
Italian	**Italijan/Italijanka**
Japanese	**Japanac/Japanka**
Pakistani	**Pakistanac/**
	Pakistanka
Russian	**Rus/Ruskinja**
Scottish	**Škotlanđanin/**
	Škotlanđanka
Turkish	**Turčin/Turkinja**
Welsh	**Velšanin/Velšanka**

Europe	**Evropa**
—European	**—Evropljanin** *m*/
	Evropljanka *f*
European Union	**Evropska Unija;**
	Evropska Zajednica

Where were you born?	**Gde ste rođeni?**
I was born in . . .	**Rođen sam u ...**

—Former Yugoslavian republics

Bosnia	**Bosna**
—Bosnian	**—Bosanac** *m*/**Bosanka** *f*
Croatia	**Hrvatska**
—Croatian	**—Hrvat/Hrvatica**
Macedonia	**Makedonija**
—Macedonian	**—Makedonac/**
	Makedonka
Montenegro	**Crna Gora**
—Montenegrin	**—Crnogorac/Crnogorka**
Serbia	**Srbija**
—Serbian	**—Srbin /Srpkinja**
Slovenia	**Slovenija**
—Slovenian	**—Slovenac/Slovenka**

c = hi*ts*   č = *ch*urch   ć = ty/*chy*   đ = *dy*   dž = *j*am

—Republics of Eastern Europe

Albania	**Albanija**
—Albanian	**—Albanac** *m*/**Albanka** *f*
Austria	**Austrija**
—Austrian	**—Austrijanac/**
	Austrijanka
Bulgaria	**Bugarska**
—Bulgarian	**—Bugarin/ Bugarka**
Czech Republic	**Češka**
—Czech	**—Čeh/Čehinja**
Hungary	**Mađarska**
—Hungarian	**—Mađar/ Mađarica**
Moldova	**Moldavija**
—Moldovan	**—Moldavac/Moldavka**
Romania	**Rumunija**
—Romanian	**—Rumun/ Rumunka**
Slovakia	**Slovačka**
—Slovakian	**—Slovak/ Slovakinja**
Slovenia	**Slovenija**
—Slovenian	**—Slovenac/Slovenka**

—Occupations

What do you do?	**Šta radite? Čime se bavite?**
I am a/an . . .	**Ja sam...**
accountant	**ekonomista**
administrator	**administrator; činovnik; službenik** *m*/ **službenica** *f*
agronomist	**agronom**
aid worker	**humanitarni radnik/ humanitarna radnica**
architect	**arhitekta**
artist	**umetnik/umetnica**
blacksmith	**kovač**

businessperson	**biznismen; poslovni preduzimač**
carpenter	**stolar**
consultant	**konsultant; savetnik/ savetnica**
dentist	**zubar/zubarka**
diplomat	**diplomata**
doctor	**doktor**
economist	**ekonomista**
engineer	**inženjer**
farmer	**farmer; poljoprivrednik**
film-maker	**filmski umetnik**
joiner	**stolar**
journalist	**novinar/novinarka**
judge	**sudija**
lawyer	**advokat**
mechanic	**mehaničar**
negotiator	**pregovarač/ posrednik**
nurse	**medicinska sestra** *f*/ **medicinski brat** *m*
observer	**posmatrač**
office worker	**službenik**
pilot	**pilot**
political scientist	**politički naučnik**
scientist	**naučnik**
secretary	**sekretar/sekretarica**
soldier	**vojnik**
student: *school*	**učenik**
university	**student**
surgeon	**hirurg**
tailor	**krojač/ šnajder**
teacher	**nastavnik/ profesor**
specialist	**specijalista**
tourist	**turista**

c = hi*ts*   č = *ch*urch   ć = t*y*/*chy*   đ = *dy*   dž = *j*am

trader	**trgovac**
writer	**pisac**

I work in . . .	**Radim u...**
an aid agency	**humanitarnoj organizaciji**
the hotel industry	**hotelskoj industriji**
industry	**industriji**
I.T.	**kompjuterskoj industriji**
the media	**medijskoj industriji**
telecommunications	**telekomunikacijama**
the tourist industry	**turističkoj industriji**

—Age

How old are you?	**Koliko imate godina?**
I am . . . years old.	**Imam... godina.**

—Family

Are you married?	m	**Jeste li oženjeni?**
	f	**Jeste li udati?**
I am not married.	m	**Nisam oženjen.**
	f	**Nisam udata.**
I am married.	m	**Oženjen sam.**
	f	**Udata sam.**
I am divorced.	m	**Razveden sam.**
	f	**Razvedena sam.**
I am a widow.		**Ja sam udovica.**
I am a widower.		**Ja sam udovac.**

Do you have a boyfriend?	**Imate/ Imaš li momka?**
Do you have a girlfriend?	**Imate/Imaš li devojku?**

What is his/her name?	**Kako se on/ona zove?**

INTRODUCTIONS

How many children do you have?	**Koliko dece imate?**
I don't have any children.	**Nemam dece.**
I have a daughter.	**Imam jednu kćerku.**
I have a son.	**Imam jednog sina.**
How many brothers do you have?	**Koliko braće imate/ imaš?**
How many sisters do you have?	**Koliko sestara imate/ imaš?**
How many brothers and sisters do you have?	**Koliko imate/imaš braće i sestara?**

—Family members

> **RELATIVES** — Serbs have strong sense of family ties and so there is a wide range of special words for relatives — distant as well as close. Only immediate family are outlined below. For details of aunts, cousins and in-laws, look up the relevant English term in the dictionary section of this book.

father	**otac**
mother	**majka**
parents	**roditelji**
grandfather	**deda**
grandmother	**baba**
granddaughter	**unuka**
grandson	**unuk**
brother	**brat**
sister	**sestra**
daughter	**kćerka**
son	**sin**
twins	**blizanci**
husband	**suprug/ muž**

c = hi*ts*   č = *ch*urch   ć = *ty/chy*   đ = *dy*   dž = *j*am

wife	**supruga/ žena**
family	**porodica**
man	**čovek**
woman	**žena**
boy	**dečak**
girl	**devojčica**
baby	**beba**
child	**dete**
children	**deca**
teenager *boy*	**tinejdžer; momak**
teenager *girl*	**tinejdžerka; devojka**
elder *old person*	**starac/starica**
person	**osoba**
people	**ljudi**
orphan	**siroče**

—Religion

What is your religion?	**Koje ste vere?** *or* **Koja je vaša veroispovest?**
I am (a) . . .	**Ja sam...**
Orthodox	**pravoslavac/ pravoslavka**
Christian	**hrišćanin/hrišćanka**
Catholic	**katolik/katolkinja**
Muslim	**musliman/muslimanka**
Buddhist	**budista**
Hindu	**indus**
Jewish	**jevrejin/jevrejka**
I am not religious.	**Nisam religiozan/ religiozna.**

4. LANGUAGE

Do you speak Serbian?	**Govorite li srpski?**
Do you know Serbian?	**Znate li srpski?**
Do you speak English?	**Govorite li engleski?**
Do you speak Arabic?	**Govorite li arapski?**
Do you speak French?	**Govorite li francuski?**
Do you speak German?	**Govorite li nemački?**
Do you speak Greek?	**Govorite li grčki?**
Do you speak Italian?	**Govorite li italijanski?**
Do you speak Russian?	**Govorite li ruski?**
Do you speak Spanish?	**Govorite li španski?**
Do you speak Turkish?	**Govorite li turski?**
Does anyone speak English?	**Da li neko govori engleski?**
Does anyone know English?	**Da li neko zna engleski?**
I know a little . . .	**Ja malo znam...**
I don't know any . . .	**Ja uopšte ne znam...**
I understand.	**Ja razumem.**
I don't understand.	**Ja ne razumem.**
Please point to the word in the book.	**(Molim vas) pokažite mi tu reč u knjizi.**
Please wait while I look up the word.	**Sačekajte dok pronađem reč.**

Could you speak more slowly, please?	**Govorite sporije, molim vas.**
Could you repeat that?	**Molim vas, ponovite.**
How do you say . . . in Serbian?	**Kako se kaže... na srpskom.**
What does . . . mean?	**Šta znači...?**
How do you pronounce this word?	**Kako se izgovara ova reč?**

I know . . .	**Ja znam/ govorim...**
Arabic	**arapski**
Armenian	**jermenski**
Chinese	**kineski**
Danish	**danski**
Dutch	**holandski**
English	**engleski**
French	**francuski**
German	**nemački**
Greek	**grčki**
Hindi	**hindi**
Italian	**italijanski**
Japanese	**japanski**
Russian	**ruski**
Spanish	**španski**
Turkish	**turski**

5. BUREAUCRACY

name		**ime**
patronym		**ime oca** or **ime roditelja**
surname		**prezime**
address		**adresa**
date of birth		**datum rođenja**
place of birth		**mesto rođenja**
nationality		**narodnost**
citizenship		**državljanstvo**
age		**starost**
(sex)	male	**muški**
	female	**ženski**
religion		**veroispovest**
reason for travel:		**razlog putovanja**
business		**posao**
tourism		**turizam**
work		**posao**
personal		**lični razlog**
profession		**zanimanje**
marital status		**bračno stanje**
single	*m*	**neoženjen**
	f	**neudata**
married	*m*	**oženjen**
	f	**udata**
divorced	*m*	**razveden**
	f	**razvedena**
date		**datum**
date of arrival		**datum dolaska**
date of departure		**datum odlaska**
passport		**pasoš**

c = hi*ts*   č = *ch*urch   ć = *ty/chy*   đ = *dy*   dž = *j*am

passport number	**broj pasoša**
visa	**viza**
currency	**valuta**

—Enquiries

Is this the correct form?	**Je li ovo pravi formular?**
What does this mean?	**Šta ovo znači?**
Where is . . . 's office?	**Gde je ... kancelarija/ služba?**
Which floor is ... on?	**Na kom se spratu nalazi...?**
Does the lift work?	**Da li radi lift?**
Is Mr./Mrs./Miss . . . in?	**Je li tu gospodin/ gospođa/gospođica...?**
Please tell him/her that I am here.	**Molim vas recite mu/ joj da sam stigao/stigla.**
I can't wait, I have an appointment.	**Ne mogu da sačekam, imam zakazan sastanak.**
Tell him/her that I was here.	**Recite mu/joj da sam dolazio/dolazila.**

—Ministries

Ministry of Defense	**Ministarstvo odbrane**
Ministry of Agriculture	**Ministarstvo privrede**
Ministry of Home Affairs	**Ministartsvo unutrašnjih poslova**
Ministry of Foreign Affairs	**Ministastvo inostranih poslova**
Ministry of Health	**Ministarstvo zdravlja**

Ministry of Education	**Ministarstvo prosvete**
Ministry of Justice	**Ministarstvo pravde**
Ministry of Culture	**Ministarstvo kulture**

Some common expressions...

Here are a few expressions you'll hear in everyday conversation:

dobro! važi!	all right!; okay!
bravo!	bravo!
jao!	alas!
mislim...; znači...	I mean...; that's to say...
šteta!	what a pity!
dosta!	enough!; well now!
nikako!	out of the question!
ništa!	not at all! *in response to 'thank you' or 'sorry'*
da!	yes!
stvarno?	really?
što da ne?; zašto da ne?	why not?
dakle...	so...; well... *used at the beginning of a sentence to signify summation or conclusion*
nema problema!	no problem!
ej!	hey!
hajde!; 'ajde!	come on!
au!	wow!
ura!	hooray!

6. TRAVEL

PUBLIC TRANSPORT — Within urban areas, the main means of public transport are buses (**autobusi**), trolley buses (**trolejbusi**) and trams (**tramvaj**), which often can be too packed for comfort, while Belgrade's metro system (see below) is being swiftly outpaced by the growth of new suburbs. Privately run buses and minibuses also exist — they are cleaner and more modern and they run exactly the same routes as the state ones and use the same pick-up points. Fares on privately run buses can be slightly higher. Longer distance travel out of town offers you the usual variety of means. There are now many car rental firms, offering you vehicles with or without drivers. Rates vary. For longer distance travel, coaches are reliable and leave from specially designated areas. Travel by rail can be slow and subject to long delays mid-journey. Generally coaches tend to be quicker than trains, but trains have a bit of nostalgia value. The terrain is not so mountainous as to make cycling down the country a problem, but it is not common to find bicycles/motorbikes for hire. However, you can buy some good ones quite cheaply.

METRO — Belgrade's metro system was opened in 1981 and is a clean, fast and easy way to get around. At the moment, there is only one main line in operation, and ten stops. Trains are relatively frequent and stop running at 11 p.m. In Belgrade there are buses on the streets of Belgrade all through the night, getting less frequent between midnight and 5 a.m.

What time does . . . leave/arrive?	U koliko sati polazi/stiže ...?
the airplane	avion
the boat	brod
the bus	autobus
the train	voz
The plane is delayed.	Avion kasni.
The plane is canceled.	Avion je otkazan.
The train is delayed.	Voz kasni.
The train is canceled.	Voz je otkazan.
How long will it be delayed?	Koliko kasni?

h = lo*ch*/*h*it   j = *y*et   š = *sh*ip   ž = a*z*ure

There is a delay of . . . minutes.	**Voz/avion kasni ... minuta.**
There is a delay of one hour/two-three-four/five hours.	**Voz/avion kasni jedan-sat/dva-tri-četri sata/pet sati.**
Excuse me, where is the ticket office?	**Izvinite, gde se prodaju karte?**
Where can I buy a ticket?	**Gde mogu da kupim kartu?**
I want to go to . . .	**Želim/hoću da idem u ...**
I need a ticket to . . .	**Treba mi karta za...**
I need . . .	**Treba mi...**
a one-way ticket	**karta u jednom pravcu**
a return ticket	**povratna karta**
first class	**karta za prvu klasu**
second class	**karta za drugu klasu**
Do I pay in dollars or in dinars?	**Da li se plaća u dolarima ili u dinarima?**
You must pay in dinars.	**Plaća se u dinarima.**
You must pay in dollars.	**Plaća se u dolarima.**
You can pay in either.	**Plaća se u bilo kojoj valuti.**
Can I reserve a place?	**Mogu li da rezervišem mesto?**
How long does the trip take?	**Koliko dugo traje putovanje?**
Is it a direct route?	**Da li se preseda?**

—Air

Is there a flight to . . . ?	**Ima li letova za...?**
When is the next flight to . . . ?	**Kada je sledeći let za...?**
How long is the flight?	**Koliko dugo traje let?**
What is the flight number?	**Koji je broj leta?**
You must check in at . . .	**Čekiranje prtljaga se vrši na...**

c = hi*ts*   č = *ch*urch   ć = *ty/chy*   d = *dy*   dž = *j*am

Is the flight delayed?	**Da li let kasni?**
How many hours is the flight delayed?	**Koliko sati kasni let?**
Is this the flight for . . . ?	**Je li ovo let za...?**
Is that the flight from . . . ?	**Je li to let iz...?**
When is the London flight arriving?	**Kada stiže let iz Londona?**
Is it on time?	**Da li stiže ne vreme?**
Is it late?	**Da li kasni?**
Do I have to change planes?	**Da li se preseda?**
Has the plane left London yet?	**Je li avion krenuo iz Londona?**
What time does the plane take off?	**U koje vreme poleće avion?**
What time do we arrive in Belgrade?	**U koje vreme slećemo u Beograd?**
excess baggage	**višak prtljaga**
international flight	**međunarodni let**
internal flight	**lokalni let**

—Bus

bus stop	**autobuska stanica**
bus station	**autobuska stanica**
Where is the bus stop/ bus station?	**Gde je autobuska stanica?**
Please take me to the bus station.	**Molim vas odvedite me do autobuske stanice.**
Which bus goes to . . . ?	**Koji autobus ide za...?**
Does this bus go to . . . ?	**Da li ovaj autobus ide za...?**
How often do buses pass by?	**Koliko često prolazi autobus?**

h = lo*ch*/*hit*   j = *y*et   š = *sh*ip   ž = a*z*ure

What time is the . . . bus?	**U koje vreme ide... autobus?**
next	**sledeći**
first	**prvi**
last	**poslednji**

Where can I get a bus to . . . ?	**Gde mogu da uhvatim autobus za...?**
When is the first bus to . . . ?	**Kada ide prvi autobus za...?**
When is the last bus to . . . ?	**Kada ide poslednji autobus za...?**
When is the next bus to . . . ?	**Kada ide sledeći autobus za...?**
Do I have to change buses?	**Da li se preseda?**

Will you let me know when we get to . . . ?	**Molim vas recite mi kad stignemo u/na...**
I want to get off at . . .	**Želim da siđem u/na/kod...**
Please let me off at the next stop.	**Želim da siđem na sledećoj stanici.**
Stop, I want to get off!	**Stanite, hoću da siđem!**
Please let me off here.	**Hoću da siđem ovde.**

How long is the journey?	**Koliko dugo traje putovanje?**
What is the fare?	**Koliko košta karta?**
I need my luggage, please.	**Želim da uzmem prtljag.**
That's my bag.	**To je moja torba.**

—Rail

Please take me to the railway station.	**Molim vas odvedite/ odvezite me do železničke stanice.**

Is this the right platform for . . . ?	**Je li ovo peron za...?**
Is there a timetable?	**Imate li red vožnje?**
Where can I buy tickets?	**Gde mogu da kupim karte?**
Which platform should I go to?	**Na koji peron treba da idem?**
platform one	**prvi peron**
platform two	**drugi peron**
The train leaves from platform . . .	**Voz kreće sa ... perona.**
Passengers must . . .	**Putnici se mole da...**
change trains.	**pređu u drugi voz.**
change platforms.	**pređu na drugi peron.**
You must change trains at . . .	**Preseda se u...**
Will the train leave on time?	**Da li voz ide na vreme?**
There will be a delay of . . . minutes.	**Voz kasni ... minuta.**
There will be a delay of one hour/two-three-four/ five hours.	**Voz kasni jedan sat/ dva-tri-četrisata/ pet sati.**

—Taxi

Taxi!	**Taksi!**
Where can I get a taxi?	**Gde mogu da nađem taksi?**
Please could you get me a taxi.	**Molim vas pozovite mi taksi.**
Can you take me to . . . ?	**Možete li me odvesti do...?**
Please take me to . . .	**Odvezite me do/u/na...?**

h = lo*ch*/*h*it   j = yet   š = *sh*ip   ž = a*z*ure

How much will it cost to . . . ?	**Koliko košta vožnja do...?**
How much?	**Koliko košta?**
To this address, please.	**Odvezite me na ovu adresu.**
Turn left.	**Skrenite levo.**
Turn right.	**Skrenite desno.**
Go straight ahead.	**Idite pravo.**
Stop!	**Stanite!**
Don't stop!	**Nemojte da stajete!**
I'm in a hurry.	**Žurim.**
Please drive more slowly!	**Molim vas vozite sporije.**
Here is fine, thank you.	**Stanite ovde, hvala.**
The next corner, please.	**Do sledećeg ugla, molim vas.**
The next street to the left.	**Sledeća ulica levo.**
The next street to the right.	**Sledeća ulica desno.**
Stop here!	**Stanite ovde!**
Stop the car, I want to get out.	**Zaustavite auto, želim da izađem.**
Please wait here.	**Molim vas sačekajte ovde.**
Please take me to the airport.	**Molim vas odvezite me do aerodroma.**

—General phrases

I want to get off at . . .	**Želim da izađem kod/na/u...**
Excuse me!	**Izvinite!**
I want to get out (of the bus).	**Želim da siđem/izađem (iz autobusa).**
These are my bags.	**Ovo je moj prtljag.** or **Ovo su moje torbe.**

Please put them there.	**Molim vas stavite ovde.**
Is this seat free?	**Je li (ovo sedište) slobodno?**
I think that's my seat.	**Mislim da je ovo moje sedište.**

—Extra words

airport	**aerodrom**
airport tax	**aerodromska taksa**
ambulance	**ambulanta**
arrivals	**dolasci**
bag	**torba**
baggage	**prtljag**
baggage counter	**prtljag**
bicycle	**bicikl**
boarding pass	**bording karta**
boat	**brod**
border	**granica**
bus stop	**autobuska stanica**
car	**auto/ kola**
check-in	**"check-in"; predaja prtljaga**
check-in counter	**(as above)**
closed	**zatvoreno**
customs	**carina**
delay	**kašnjenje**
departures	**odlasci**
emergency exit	**požarni izlaz**
entrance	**ulaz**
exit	**izlaz**
express	**ekspres**
ferry	**feribot/trajekt**
(to go) on foot	**ići peške**
frontier	**granica**
helicopter	**helikopter**

horse	**konj**
information	**informacije**
local	**lokalni**
lorry	**kamion**
luggage	**prtljag**
motorbike	**motor**
no entry	**zabranjen ulaz**
no smoking	**zabranjeno pušenje**
open	**otvoreno**
path	**staza**
platform number	**broj perona**
railway	**železnica**
reserved	**rezervisano**
radio taxi	**radio taksi**
road	**put**
sign	**znak**
sleeping car	**spavaća kola**
station	**stanica**
bus station	**autobuska stanica**
train station	**železnička stanica**
telephone	**telefon**
ticket office	**prodaja karata**
timetable	**red vožnje**
toilet(s)	**toalet**
town center	**centar grada**
trolleybus	**trolejbus**
truck	**kamion**
van	**kombi**

7. ACCOMMODATION

The hotel and guesthouse network in Serbia and Montenegro is rapidly being developed. Should adequate accommodation be found away from the major towns, you will find that room service is not available, and breakfast or other meals will have to be negotiated and paid for separately. (This is very rare — maybe only in very dingy and remote, improvised guesthouses where it's not wise to stay anyway.) An excellent option in more rural areas is to have your accommodation arranged at a private house, where traditional hospitality will guarantee that you are well looked after and, as always in Serbia, well fed. More and more places are starting to offer details of their services and location on the internet, as well as offering facilities for payment by credit card.

Where can I find a hotel?	**Gde mogu da nađem hotel/smeštaj?**
I am looking for a hotel.	**Tražim hotel/smeštaj.**
Is there anywhere I can stay for the night?	**Gde mogu da odsednem večeras/ jednu noć.**
Where is . . .	**Gde je...**
a cheap hotel	**jeftin hotel**
a good hotel	**dobar hotel**
a nearby hotel	**najbliži hotel**
a clean hotel	**čist/uredan hotel**
What is the address?	**Koja je adresa?**
Could you write the address please?	**Možete li da mi zapišete adresu?**

—At the hotel

Do you have any rooms free?	**Imate li slobodnu sobu?**
I would like . . .	**Treba mi...**
a single room	**jednokrevetna soba**
a double room	**dvokrevetna soba**
We'd like a room.	**Treba nam soba.**
We'd like two rooms.	**Trebaju nam dve sobe.**

h = lo*ch*/*h*it   j = *y*et   š = *sh*ip   ž = a*z*ure

ACCOMMODATION

I want a room with . . .	**Treba mi soba sa...**
a bathroom	**kupatilom**
a shower	**tuš-kabinom**
a television	**televizorom**
a window	**prozorom**
a double bed	**duplim/bračnim krevetom**
a balcony	**balkonom**
a view	**pogledom**
I want a room that's quiet.	**Treba mi mirna soba.**
How long will you be staying?	**Koliko ostajete?**
How many nights?	**Koliko noći?**
I'm going to stay for . . .	**Ostajem...**
one day	**jedan dan**
two days	**dva dana**
one week	**nedelju dana**
Do you have any I.D. (passport)?	**Imate li identifikaciju (pasoš)?**
Sorry, we're full.	**Žao mi je, prepuni smo/ nemamo slobodnih soba.**
I have a reservation.	**Imam rezervaciju.**
We have a reservation.	**Imamo rezervaciju.**
My name is . . .	**Moje ime je...**
May I speak to the manager please?	**Mogu li da vidim menadžera/šefa?**
I have to meet someone here.	**Imam (zakazan) sastanak ovde.**
How much is it per night?	**Koliko košta (smeštaj) za jednu noć?**
How much is it per week?	**Koliko košta (smeštaj) za nedelju dana?**
How much is it per person?	**Koliko košta po osobi?**

c = hi**ts**   č = **ch**ur**ch**   ć = t**y**/**chy**   đ = **dy**   dž = **j**am

It's . . . per day.	. . . dnevno.
It's . . . per week.	. . . nedeljno.
It's . . . per person.	. . . po osobi.
Can I see the room?	Mogu li da pogledam sobu?
Are there any others?	Imate li nešto drugo?
Is there . . . ?	Da li postoji...?
airconditioning	klima uređaj
a telephone	telefon
hot water	topla voda
laundry service	vešernica
room service	lična usluga
No, I don't like it.	Ne, ne sviđa mi se.
It's too . . .	Previše je...
cold	hladno
hot	vruće
big	veliko
dark	tamno
small	malo
noisy	bučno
dirty	prljavo
It's fine, I'll take it.	U redu je, uzimam.
Where is the bathroom?	Gde je kupatilo?
Is there hot water all day?	Ima li tople vode ceo dan?
Do you have a safe?	Imate li sef?
Is there anywhere to wash clothes?	Gde mogu da operem veš?
Can I use the telephone?	Mogu li da se poslužim telefonom?

—Needs

I need candles.	Trebaju mi sveće.
I need toilet paper.	Treba mi toalet papir.

I need soap.	**Treba mi sapun.**
I need clean sheets.	**Treba mi čista posteljina.**
I need an extra blanket.	**Treba mi dodatno ćebe.**
I need drinking water.	**Treba mi voda za piće.**
I need a light bulb.	**Treba mi sijalica.**
Please change the sheets.	**Molim vas promenite posteljinu.**
I can't open the window.	**Ne mogu da otvorim prozor.**
I can't close the window.	**Ne mogu da zatvorim prozor.**
I have lost my key.	**Izgubio/igubila sam ključ.**
Can I have the key to my room?	**Mogu li dobiti ključ za moju sobu.**
The toilet won't flush.	**Ne radi kazanče.**
The water has been cut off.	**Nestala je voda.**
The electricity has been cut off.	**Nestala je struja.**
There is no gas.	**Nestao je plin.**
The heating has been cut off.	**Nestalo je grejanje.**
The heater doesn't work.	**Ne radi grejanje.**
The air conditioning doesn't work.	**Ne radi klima uređaj.**
The phone doesn't work.	**Ne radi telefon.**
I can't flush the toilet.	**Ne mogu da pustim vodu u ve-ceu.**
The toilet is blocked.	**Ve-ce je zapušen.**
I can't switch off the tap.	**Ne mogu da zatvorim slavinu.**
Where is the plug socket?	**Gde je utikač?**
wake-up call	**buđenje**

Could you please wake me up at one/two-three-four/five o'clock?	**Molim vas probudite me u jedan sat/dva-tri-četri sata/pet sati?**
I am leaving now.	**Ja idem sada.**
We are leaving now.	**Mi idemo sada.**
May I pay the bill now?	**Mogu li da platim račun?**
May we pay the bill now?	**Možemo li da platimo račun?**

—Extra words

bathroom	**kupatilo**
bed	**krevet**
blanket	**ćebe**
candle	**sveća**
candles	**sveće**
chair	**stolica**
cold water	**hladna voda**
cupboard	**kredenac**
door	**vrata**
doorlock	**brava**
electricity	**struja**
floor story	**sprat**
fridge	**frižider**
hot water	**topla voda**
key	**ključ**
lamp	**lampa**
laundry service	**vešernica**
light *electric*	**struja**
mattress	**dušek**
meal	**obrok**
meals	**obroci**
mirror	**ogledalo**
name	**ime**
noisy	**bučno**

padlock		**katanac**
pillow		**jastuk**
plug	*bath*	**čep**
	electric	**utikač**
quiet		**tiho; mirno**
quilt		**jorgan; pokrivač**
roof		**krov**
room		**soba**
room number		**broj sobe**
sheet		**čaršav**
shelf		**polica**
shower		**tuš**
stairs		**stepenice**
suitcase		**stepenište**
surname		**prezime**
table		**sto**
towel		**peškir**
veranda		**terasa**
wall		**zid**
water		**voda**
window		**prozor**

8. FOOD & DRINK

Food plays an important part of Serbian life, and important events in all aspects of life and the year are marked with a feast of one form or another. Food is a very important part of hospitality — it is both the host's duty to make sure his guests are eating and the guest's duty to partake of what is offered. Serbian cuisine is one of the world's wonders and in normal times, at homes or in restaurants, you will be offered a dazzling variety of dishes, delicacies and drinks, which vary from area to area and from season to season. Any menu you may encounter may be also written in English.

breakfast	**doručak**
lunch	**ručak**
dinner/supper	**večera**
dessert	**dezert**

—Restaurants

I'm hungry.	**Gladan/Gladna sam.**
I'm thirsty.	**Žedan/Žedna sam.**
Are you hungry?	**Vi ste gladni?**
Are you thisty?	**Vi ste žedni?**
Do you know a good restaurant?	**Da li znate neki dobar restoran?**
Do you have a table, please?	**Imate li slobadan sto?**
I would like a table for one/two/three/four people, please.	**Treba mi sto za jednu/ dve/tri/četri osobe.**
Can I see the menu please?	**Mogu li da vidim jelovnik/meni.**
I'm still looking at the menu.	**Još čitam jelovnik/meni.**

h = lo*ch*/*h*it   j = *y*et   š = *sh*ip   ž = a*z*ure

I would like to order now.	**Mogu da naručim.**
What's this?	**Šta je ovo?**
Is it spicy?	**Jel' ljuto?**
Does it have meat in it?	**Jel' s mesom?**
Do you have . . . ?	**Imate li...?**
We don't have . . .	**Nemamo...**
What would you recommend?	**Šta preporučujete?**
Do you want . . . ?	**Želite li...?**
Can I order some more . . . ?	**Mogu li da naručim još...?**
That's all, thank you.	**To je sve, hvala.**
That's enough, thanks.	**Dovoljno je, hvala.**
I haven't finished yet.	**Nisam još završio.**
I have finished eating.	**Završio/ završila sam.**
I am full up!	**Sit sam!**
Where are the toilets?	**Gde je toalet.**
I am a vegetarian.	**Ja sam vegetarijanac.**
I don't eat meat.	**Ne jedem meso.**
I don't eat chicken or fish.	**Ne jedem piletinu i ribu.**
I don't drink alcohol.	**Ne pijem (alkoholna pića).**
I don't smoke.	**Ne pušim.**
I would like . . .	**(Molim vas) donesite mi...**
an ashtray	**pepeljaru**
the bill	**račun**
a glass of water	**cašu vode**
a bottle of water	**flašu vode**
another bottle	**još jednu flašu**
a bottle opener	**otvarač za flaše**
a corkscrew	**otvarač za flaše**
dessert	**dezert**

c = hi*ts*   č = *ch*urch   ć = *ty/chy*   d = *dy*   dž = *j*am

a drink	piće
a chair	stolicu
a plate	tanjir
a glass	čašu
a cup	šolju
a napkin	salvetu
a fork	viljušku
a knife	nož
the menu	jelovnik/meni
a jug	bokal
a spoon	kašiku
a teaspoon	kašičicu
a toothpick	čačkalicu
the sugar bowl	šećer
salt	so
pepper	biber

—Tastes & textures

Genders of adjectives are given only where sound changes or irregularities occur; otherwise add **-a** to create feminine forms and **-o** to create neuter forms.

fresh	svež (-a/-e)
raw	svež; sirov
cooked	kuvani
ripe	zreo (zrela/zrelo)
tender	mek
tough meat	tvrdo meso
spicy (hot)	ljut; začinjen
stale bread	bajat hleb
sour	kiseo (kisela/kiselo)
sweet	sladak (slatka/slatko)
bitter	gorak (gorka/gorko)
hot	vruć (-a/-e)
cold	hladan (hladna/hladno)
salty	slan

taste	**ukus**
tasteless	**bezukusan (bezukusna/ bezukusno)**
tasty	**ukusan (ukusna/ukusno)**
bad/spoiled	**pokvaren**
too much	**previše**
too little	**premalo**
not enough	**nedovoljno**
empty	**prazan (prazna/prazno)**
full	**pun**
good	**dobar (dobra/dobro)**

—General food words

burger		**burger; pljeskavica**
butter		**puter; maslac**
bread:	flat	**hleb; pogača**
	loaf	**vekna hleba**
cake		**kolač**
candy		**bonbona**
cheese		**sir**
cottage cheese		**beli sir**
chewing gum		**žvaka; žvakaća guma**
egg		**jaje**
boiled egg		**kuvano jaje**
flour		**brašno**
french fries		**pomfrit; prženi krompir**
garlic		**beli luk**
ginger		**đumbir**
honey		**med**
ice-cream		**sladoled**
jam; jelly		**džem; žele; slatko**
ketchup		**kečup; paradajz sos**
mint		**menta; nana**
mustard		**senf**
nut		**orah**
almond		**badem**

hazel		**lešnik**
pistachio		**pistaćo**
walnut		**orah**
oil		**ulje**
pasta		**testenine; makaroni**
pepper:	black pepper	**crni biber**
	hot pepper	**ljuta paprika/papričica; feferoni**
	sweet pepper	**biber**
pizza		**pica**
provisions		**zalihe**
rice		**pirinač; riža**
salad		**salata**
salt		**so**
sandwich		**sendvič**
sauce		**sos**
shopping		**namirnice**
soup		**supa**
spice		**začin**
sugar		**šećer**
syrup		**sirup**
tablecloth		**stoljnjak**
tray		**poslužavnik**
teapot		**čajnik**
vinegar		**sirće**
yogurt		**jogurt**

▬Vegetables

aubergine	**plavi patlidžan**
beans	**pasulj**
green beans	**boranija**
beet; beetroot	**cvekla**
cabbage	**kupus**
carrot	**šargarepa**
cauliflower	**karfiol**
chickpeas	**leblebije**

FOOD & DRINK

cucumber	**krastavac**
eggplant	**plavi patlidžan**
lentils	**sočivo**
lettuce	**zelena salata**
onion	**crni luk**
peas	**grašak**
pepper	**paprika**
potatoes	**krompir**
pumpkin	**tikva; bundeva**
radish	**rotkvice**
salad	**salata**
spinach	**spanać; špinat; blitva**
tomato	**paradajz**
vegetables *ready to eat*	**sveže povrće**

> **PICKLES** — Due to the seasonal use of vegetables, winter salads (**zimnica**) consist of pickles such as **kiseli krastavčići** (pickled gerkins), **kiseli kupus** (sauerkraut), **kisele paprke** (pickled peppers) and **ajvar** (vegetable preserves).

—Fruit

almond	**badem**
apple	**jabuka**
apricot	**kajsija**
banana	**banana**
blackberry	**kupina**
blueberry	**borovnica**
cherry	**trešnja**
sour cherry	**višnja**
date	**urma**
fig	**smokva**
fruit	**voće**
grapefruit	**grejpfrut**
grapes	**grožđe**
lemon/lime	**limun**
melon	**dinja**

c = hi*ts*   č = *ch*urch   ć = *ty/chy*   d = *dy*   dž = *j*am

mulberry	**dud**
orange	**pomorandža**
peach	**breskva**
pear	**kruška**
plum	**šljiva**
pomegranate	**nar**
quince	**dunja**
raisins	**suvo grozđe**
raspberry	**malina**
strawberry	**jagoda**
watermelon	**lubenica; bostan**

Snacks . . .

As most Serbs traditionally work from 7 a.m. till 3 p.m., they tend to snack at about 10-11 a.m. and have lunch after 3 p.m. Kiosks or stands selling sweet and savory pastries are therefore out on the streets during the day. In the afternoon they are replaced by kiosks selling popcorn, French fries and/or a selection of snacks such as roasted peanuts, sunflower seeds and pumpkin seeds. These are mainly located in pedestrian areas and near leisure and entertainment centres — Serbs like to take walks out on the town in the late afternoon/early evening, browsing through shops or meeting friends. A very popular snack which every vistor is urged to try is **burek** — a rich pastry flled with cheese, meat or vegetables. It is eaten at almost any time of day but is particularly popular as a snack at the end of a night out drinking or for breakfast, when it is often accompanied with a yogurt drink.

—Meat

beef	**teletina**
chicken	**piletina**
fat (noun)	**mast**
fish	**riba**
goat meat	**jaretina**
kebab	**ćevap; ćevapi; ćevapčiči**
lamb *meat*	**jagnjetina**
meat	**meso**

FOOD & DRINK

—Drinks

alcohol	**alkohol**
alcoholic drinks	**alkoholna pića**
beer	**pivo**
bottle	**flaša**
can	**limenka; konzerva**
coffee	**kafa**
coffee with milk	**bela kafa**
fruit juice	**voćni sok**
ice	**led**
milk	**mleko**
mineral water	**mineralna voda; kisela voda**
spirits	**žestoka pića**
tea	**čaj**
tea with milk	**čaj s mlekom**
tea with lemon	**čaj s limunom**
no sugar, please!	**bez šećera, molim!**
water	**voda**
wine	**vino**
red	**crno vino**
white	**belo vino**

9. DIRECTIONS

Where is . . . ?	Gde je... ?
the academy	akademija
the airport	aerodrom
the art gallery	umetnička galerija
a bank	banka
the cathedral	katedrala
the church	crkva
the city center	centar grada
the consulate	konzulat
the . . . embassy	...ska ambasada
the . . . faculty	... fakultet
the hotel	hotel
the information office	informacije
the main square	glavni trg
the market	pijaca
the ministry of . . .	ministarstvo...
the monastery	manastir
the mosque	džamija
the museum	muzej
parliament	skupština/parlament
the police station	policijska stanica
the post office	pošta
the railway station	železnička stanica
public telephone	telefonska govornica
the toilet(s)	toalet
the university	univerzitet

What . . . is this?	Koji/koja/koje je ovo...?
bridge	most
building	zgrada
city	grad
district	oblast
river	reka

h = loch/hit   j = yet   š = ship   ž = azure

DIRECTIONS

road	**put**
street	**ulica**
town	**grad**
village	**selo**

What is this building?	**Koja je ovo zgrada?**
What is that building?	**Koja je ono zgrada?**
What time does it open?	**U koliko sati se otvara?**
What time does it close?	**U koliko sati se zatvara?**

Can I park here?	**Mogu li da se parkiram ovde?**
Are we on the right road for . . . ?	**Jesmo li na pravom putu za...?**
How many kilometers is it to . . . ?	**Još koliko kilometara do...?**
It is . . . kilometers away.	**Još ... kilometara.**
How far is the next village?	**Još koliko do najbližeg sela?**
Where can I find this address?	**Kako mogu da dođem do ove adrese?**
Can you show me on the map?	**Pokažite mi na mapi.**
How do I get to . . . ?	**Kako se ide do...?**
I need to go to . . .	**Treba da dođem do...**
Can I walk there?	**Mogu li da stignem peške?**
Is it far?	**Jel' daleko?**
Is it near?	**Jel' blizu?**
Is it far from here?	**Jel' daleko odavde?**
Is it near here?	**Jel' blizu odavde?**
It is not far.	**Nije daleko.**

Go straight ahead.	**Idite pravo.**
Turn left.	**Skrenite levo.**
Turn right.	**Skrenite desno.**
to the left	**s leva**
to the right	**s desna**
to one side	**sa strane**
at the next corner	**kod sledećeg ugla**
at the traffic lights	**kod semafora**
behind	**iza**
far	**daleko**
in front	**ispred**
left	**levo**
near	**blizu**
opposite *across the road*	**preko puta**
outside	**ispred**
right	**desno**
straight on	**pravo**
under	**ispod**
bridge	**most**
corner	**ugao; ćošak**
crossroads	**raskrsnica**
cul-de-sac	**slepa ulica**
one-way street	**jednosmerna ulica**

—Points of the compass

north	**sever**
adjective	**severni**
south	**jug**
adjective	**južni**
west	**zapad**
adjective	**zapadni**
east	**istok**
adjective	**istočni**

10. SHOPPING

> **MARKETS** — For fresh produce go to a **pijaca**, or big market. Prices and availability of goods are seasonal. As a foreigner, you may occasionally find yourself paying a little more here —but not much! The best time is early morning when everything is at its freshest, particularly for meat and fish. Many local delicacies can be found here, including yogurts and cheeses, smoked meats, and an array of spices, nuts and berries. In Belgrade, visit the colorful Zeleni Venac market on a slope above the Railway and Central Bus Station or the Bajlonova Pijaca market — places where you can buy all the usual produce plus consumer products at a bargain, from cigarettes to C.D./D.V.D.-players, from clothing to handicrafts.

Where can I find a . . . ?	**Gde mogu da nađem...?**
Where can I buy . . . ?	**Gde mogu da kupim...?**
Where's the market?	**Gde je pijaca?**
Where's the nearest . . . ?	**Gde je najbliži/-a/-e...?**
Can you help me?	**Pomozite mi, molim vas.**
Can I help you?	**Izvol'te?** or **Kako mogu da vam pomognem?**
I'm just looking.	**Samo razgledam.**
I'd like to buy . . .	**Želim da kupim...**
Could you show me some . . . ?	**Pokažite mi...**
Can I look at it?	**Mogu li da pogledam?**
Do you have any . . . ?	**Imate li...?**
This.	**Ovo.**
That.	**To.**
I don't like it.	**Ne sviđa mi se.**
I like it.	**Sviđa mi se.**
Do you have anything cheaper?	**Imate li nešto jeftinije?**
cheaper/better	**jeftinije/kvalitetnije**
larger/smaller	**veće/manje**

c = hi*ts*   č = *ch*urch   ć = *ty/chy*   đ = *dy*   dž = *j*am

Do you have anything else?	**Imate li nešto drugo?**
Sorry, that's all we have.	**Žao mi je to je sve što imamo.**
I'll take this...	**Uzeću ovaj/ovu/ovo....**
How much/many do you want?	**Koliko (komada) želite?**
How much is it?	**Koliko košta?**
Can you write down the price?	**Napišite mi cenu, molim vas.**
Could you lower the price?	**Jel' može jeftinije?**
I don't have much money.	**Nemam puno para.**
Do you take credit cards?	**Da li primate kreditnu karticu?**
Would you like it wrapped?	**Želite li da vam zavijem?**
Will that be all?	**Jel' to sve?**
Thank you, goodbye.	**Hvala, doviđenja.**
I want to return this.	**Želim da vratim ovo.**

—Outlets

auto supply store	**prodavnica auto delova**
baker's	**pekara**
bank	**banka**
barber shop	**berber; frizer**
I'd like a haircut please.	**Šišanje molim.**
bookshop	**knjižara**
bureau de change	**menjačnica**
butcher's	**mesara**
pharmacy	**apoteka**
photographer's	**fotograf**
clothes shop	**prodavnica odeće**
dairy products store	**prodavnica mlečnih proizvoda**
dentist	**zubar**
department store	**robna kuća**

SHOPPING

dressmaker	**krojač; šnajder**
electrical goods store	**prodavnica električnih uređaja**
florist	**cvećara**
greengrocer	**piljara**
hairdresser	**frizer**
hospital	**bolnica**
kiosk	**kiosk**
laundrette	**vešernica**
market	**pijaca**
newsstand	**trafika; kiosk**
shoe repairs	**šuster; obućar**
shoe store	**prodavnica cipela; prodavnica obuće**
shop	**prodavnica**
souvenir shop	**prodavnica suvenira**
stationery store	**knjižara**
supermarket	**samoposluga; samousluga; supermarket**
travel agent	**putna agencija**
vegetable shop	**piljara**
watchmaker's	**časovničar**

—Gifts

boots	**čizme**
box	**kutija; kutijica**
bracelet	**narukvica**
candlestick	**svećnjak**
cap	**kapa; kačket**
fur cap	**šubara**
carpet	**tepih**
chain	**lanac**
chest *box*	**sanduk**
clock	**(zidni) sat**

copper	*noun*	**bakar**
	adjective	**bakarni**
crystal	*noun*	**kristal**
	adjective	**kristalni**
curtains		**zavese**
cushion		**jastuče**
earrings		**minđuše**
gold	*noun*	**zlato**
	adjective	**zlatan (zlatna/zlatno)**
handicraft		**ručni rad**
hat		**šešir**
iron		**gvožđe; gvozden**
jewelry		**nakit**
leather	*noun*	**koža**
	adjective	**kožni**
metal	*noun*	**metal**
	adjective	**metalni**
modern		**moderan (moderna/ moderno)**
necklace		**orglica**
pottery		**grnčarija**
ring		**prsten**
rosary		**brojanica**
scarf		**marama**
silver	*noun*	**srebro**
	adjective	**srebrni**
steel	*noun*	**čelik**
	adjective	**čelični**
stone	*noun*	**kamen**
	adjective	**kameni**
traditional		**tradicionalni**
vase		**vaza**
watch		**(ručni) sat**
wood	*noun*	**drvo**
	adjective	**drveni**

—Clothes

bag; handbag	torba; tašna
belt	kaiš
boot	čizma
boots	čizme
rubber boots	gumene čizme
bra; brassiere	brus-halter
bracelet	narukvica
button	dugme
buttonhole	otvor za dugme
cloth	tkanina
clothes	odeća
coat	kaput
collar	kragna
cotton	pamuk
dress	haljina
fabric	tkanina
gloves	rukavice
handbag	tašna
handkerchief	maramica
heel	štikla
jacket	jakna
jumper	džemper
leather	koža
material	materijal
necktie	kravata, mašna
overcoat	kaput
pin	igla
pocket	džep
sandals	sandale
scarf	šal; marama
scissors	makaze
shawl	šal; ogrtač
shirt	košulja
shoes	cipele
silk	svila

c = hits   č = church   ć = ty/chy   đ = dy   dž = jam

silken	**svileni**
socks	**čarape**
sole of shoe	**đon**
stick: walking stick	**štap**
suit of clothes	**odelo**
sweater	**džemper**
thread	**konac**
tie; necktie	**kravata; mašna**
tights	**čarape**
trousers	**pantalone**
umbrella	**kišobran**
underwear	**donji veš**
waistcoat	**prsluk**
walking stick	**štap**
wool *noun*	**vuna**
adjective	**vuneni**
zipper	**rajsferšlus; zip**

—Toiletries

aspirin	**aspirin**
brush	**četka**
comb	**češalj**
condom	**kondom**
cotton wool	**vata**
deodorant	**dezodorans**
hairbrush	**četka za kosu**
lipstick	**karmin**
mascara	**maskara**
nail-clippers	**grickalica za nokte**
nail-polish	**lak za nokte**
perfume	**parfem**
powder	**puder**
razor *electric*	**električni brijač;**
	mašina za brijanje
razorblade	**žilet; brijač**
safety pin	**zihernadla**

h = lo*ch*/*h*it   j = *y*et   š = *sh*ip   ž = a*z*ure

shampoo	**šampon**
shaving cream	**pena za brijanje**
sleeping pills	**tablete za spavanje**
soap	**sapun**
sponge	**sunđer**
sunblock cream	**krema za sunčanje**
thermometer	**termometar**
tissues	**maramice**
toilet paper	**toalet papir**
toothbrush	**četkica za zube**
toothpaste	**pasta za zube**
toothpick	**čačkalica**

—Stationery

ballpoint	**hemijska olovka**
book	**knjiga**
dictionary	**rečnik**
envelope	**koverat**
guidebook	**vodič**
ink	**mastilo**
magazine	**časopis; magazin; žurnal**
map	**mapa**
road map	**putna mapa**
a map of Belgrade	**mapa Beograda**
newspaper	**novine**
a newspaper in English	**novine na engleskom**
notebook	**sveska**
novel	**roman**
a novel in English	**roman na engleskom**
paper	**papir**
a piece of paper	**parče papira**
pen	**olovka**
pencil	**drvena; grafitna olovka**
postcard	**razglednica**
scissors	**makaze**
writing paper	**papir za pisanje**

c = hi*ts*   č = *ch*urch   ć = *ty/chy*   đ = *dy*   dž = *j*am

Do you have any foreign publications?

Imate li publikacije na stranim jezicima?

—Photography

How much is it to process (and print) this film?

Koliko košta razvijanje filma i izrada slika?

When will the photos be ready?

Kada će biti gotove slike?

I'd like film for this camera.

Treba mi film za ovaj aparat.

black and white film	**crno beli film**
camera	**aparat**
color film	**film u boji**
film	**film**
flash	**blic**
lens	**sočivo**
light meter	**merač osvetljenja**

—Electrical equipment

> For hi-tech stuff like cassettes, videos/video-players or transformers, C.D. and D.V.D. players, computers and computer games, you are more likely to be understood if you use the English terms.

adapter	**adapter; transformator**
battery	**baterija**
cassette	**kaseta**
C.D.	**ce de**
C.D. player	**ce de**
fan	**ventilator**
hairdryer	**fen za kosu**
iron (for clothing)	**pegla**
kettle	**katao**
plug *electric*	**utikač**

h = lo*ch*/*h*it   j = yet   š = *sh*ip   ž = a*z*ure

portable T.V.	**portabl te ve**
radio	**radio**
record	**ploča**
tape (cassette)	**traka (kaseta)**
tape recorder	**kasetofon**
television	**televizija**
transformer	**transformator**
video (player)	**video**
videotape	**video traka**

—Sizes

small	**mali**
big	**veliki**
heavy	**težak (teška/teško)**
light	**lak**
more	**više**
less	**manje**
many	**mnogo**
too much/many	**previše**
enough	**dovoljno**
That's enough.	**Dovoljno je!**
a little bit	**malo**
also	**takođe**

Do you have a carrier bag?	**Imate li kesu?**

11. WHAT'S TO SEE

Do you have a guidebook?	**Imate li vodič*?**
Do you have a local map?	**Imate li lokalnu mapu/ mapu grada?**
Is there a guide who speaks English?	**Imate li vodiča* koji govori engleski?**

What are the main attractions?	**Šta su glavne znamenitosti/atrakcije?**
What is that?	**Šta je to?**
How old is it?	**Koliko ima godina?**
May I take a photograph?	**Mogu li da slikam?**

What time does it open?	**U koliko sati se otvara?**
What time does it close?	**U koliko sati se zatvara?**
Is there an entrance fee?	**Da li se naplaćuje ulaz?**
How much?	**Koliko košta?**

What is this monument/ statue?	**Koji je ovo spomenik?; Koja je ovo statua/bista?**
Who is that statue of?	**Čija je ova statua/bista?**

What's there to do in the evening?	**Gde može da se izađe uveče?**

Are there any nightclubs/ discos?	**Ima li nekih noćnih klubova/ diskoteka?**

Is there a concert?	**Ima li neki koncert?**
How much does it cost to get in?	**Koliko košta ulaz?**

*Note that **vodič** is used to mean "guide" both as book and person.

When is the wedding?	**Kada je svadba?**
What time does it begin?	**U koliko sati počinje?**
Can we swim here?	**Možemo li da plivamo ovde?**
classical music	**klasična muzika**
concert	**koncert**
dancing	**ples**
disco	**disko; diskoteka**
disc jockey	**di džej**
elevator	**lift**
escalator	**pokretne stepenice**
exhibition	**izložba**
folk dancing	**kolo, folklor**
folk music	**folk muzika; narodna muzika**
jazz	**džez**
lift	**lift**
nightclub	**noćni klub**
opera	**opera**
party	**žurka**
pop music	**pop muzika**

Bars & cafés . . .

A **kafana** is a traditional tavern with food; a **kafić** is a café which also serves alcoholic drinks and stays open throughout the night; a **bar** is like a **kafić** but bigger. People tend to go on café/bar-crawls more so then spending the whole night in a nightclub. You will also find the odd traditional English/Irish pubs.

—Buildings

academy of sciences	**akademija nauka**
apartment	**stan**
apartment building	**zgrada**

archaeological	**arheološki**
art gallery	**(umetnička) galerija**
bakery	**pekara**
bar	**bar, kafić**
(apartment) block	**zgrada**
building	**zgrada**
casino	**kazino**
castle	**tvrđava**
cathedral	**katedrala**
cemetery	**groblje**
church	**crkva**
cinema	**bioskop**
city map	**mapa grada**
college	**koledž**
concert hall	**koncertna dvorana**
convent	**manastir**
embassy	**ambasada**
hospital	**bolnica**
house	**kuća**
housing estate/project	**naselje**
library	**biblioteka**
main square	**glavni trg**
market	**pijaca**
monastery	**manastir**
monument	**spomenik**
mosque	**džamija**
museum	**muzej**
old city	**stari grad**
opera house	**opera**
park	**park**
parliament	**parlament**
restaurant	**restoran**
ruins	**ruševine**
school	**škola**
shop	**prodavnica**
shrine	**svetilište**

stadium	**stadion**
statue	**statua**
store	**prodavnica**
street	**ulica**
tea house	**čajdžinica; kafana; kafić**
temple	**hram**
theater	**pozorište**
tomb	**grob**
tower	**kula**
university	**univerzitet**
zoo	**zoološki vrt**

—Occasions

birth	**rođenje**
death	**smrt**
funeral	**sahrana**
wedding	**svadba**

12. FINANCE

> **CURRENCY** — The national currency is the **dinar** (1 Yugoslav New Dinar = 100 **paras**), which comes in bills of various denominations between 10 and 5,000. However, euros are also accepted in many places. It is always best to change to local currency at one of the money exchanges (**menjačnica**)which have mushroomed over the last few years. These often have more favorable exchange rates than banks. Bills may be refused it they are creased, torn, old or simply a low denomination. Also, if you're paying with **dinars**, avoid taking large bills as you might have difficulty getting them changed when out shopping. Banks are open between 8 a.m. and 3 p.m. everyday from Monday to Friday but the **menjačnicas** are open until late in the evening seven days a week. The cashiers will often know a European language or two, and almost all will show the workings of the exchange on a calculator for you and give you a receipt. Many shops and kiosks will also be happy to change money for you — but it is better to avoid having to do this.

I want to change some dollars.	**Želim da promenim dolare.**
I want to change some euros.	**Želim da promenim evro.**
I want to change some pounds.	**Želim da promenim funte.**
I want to buy some dinars.	**Želim da kupim dinare.**
Where can I change some money?	**Gde mogu da promenim novac/kupim dinare?**
What is the exchange rate?	**Koji je kurs?**
What is the commission?	**Kolika je provizija?**
Could you please check that again?	**Molim vas proverite ponovo?**
Could you write that down for me?	**Molim vas zapišite mi.**

h = loch/hit   j = yet   š = ship   ž = azure

Can I use your calculator?	**Mogu li da pozajmim digitron?**
dinar	**dinar**
dollar	**dolar**
euro	**evro**
pound (sterling)	**funta**
bank notes	**novčanice**
calculator	**digitron**
cash dispenser/point	**bankomat**
cashier	**kasa**
coins	**novčići; novac u metalu**
credit card	**kreditna kartica**
commission	**provizija**
exchange; bureau de change	**menjačnica**
exchange rate	**kurs**
(loose) change	**kusur**
receipt	**račun**
signature	**potpis**

13. COMMUNICATIONS

Where is the post office?	**Gde je pošta?**
When does the post office open?	**Kada se otvara pošta?**
When does the post office close?	**Kada se zatvara pošta?**
Where is the mailbox?	**Gde je poštansko sanduče?**
Is there any mail for me?	**Ima li pošte za mene?**
How long will it take for this to get there?	**Koliko vremena treba da ovo stigne?**
How much does it cost to send this to . . . ?	**Koliko košta da se ovo pošalje u...?**
I need some stamps.	**Trebaju mi poštanske markice.**
I would like to send ...	**Želim da pošaljem...**
a letter	**pismo**
a postcard	**razglednicu**
a parcel	**paket**
a telegram	**telegram**
air mail	**avionska pošta**
envelope	**koverat**
mailbox	**poštansko sanduče**
to parcel up	**spakovati**
registered mail	**preporučena pošta**
stamp	**poštanska markica**

—Tele-etiquette

I would like to make a phone call.	**Treba mi telefon.** *or* **Želim da telefoniram.**

Where is the telephone?	**Gde je telefon?**
May I use your phone?	**Mogu li da se poslužim vašim telefonom?**
Can I telephone from here?	**Mogu li da telefoniram odavde?**
Can you help me get this number?	**Pomozite mi da nazovem ovaj broj.**
Can I dial direct?	**Mogu li direktno da biram?**
May I speak to . . . ?	**Mogu li dobiti...?** *or* **Dajte mi...**
Can I have the extension...	**Dajte mi lokal...**
Can I leave a message?	**Mogu li da ostavim poruku?**
Who is calling?	**Ko je to?** *or* **Ko je na telefonu?**
Who are you calling?	**Ko vam treba?**
Can I take your name?	**Kako se zovete?**
Which number are you dialing?	**Koji broj vam treba?**
He/She is not here at the moment — would you like to leave a message?	**On/ona nije tu trenutno — želite li da ostavite poruku?**
This is not . . .	**Nije ovo...**
You are mistaken.	**To je greška.**
You've got the wrong number.	**Dobili ste pogrešan broj.**
This is the . . . office.	**Ovo je ... služba.**
Hello, I need to speak to . . .	**Dobar dan, treba mi...**
I am calling this number . . .	**Treba mi broj...**

c = hi*ts* č = *ch*urch ć = *ty/chy* đ = *dy* dž = *j*am

COMMUNICATIONS

Please phone me.	**Molim vas javite se/ telefonirajte mi.**
Send me a text message!	**Pošaljite mi tekst poruku/es em es.**
The telephone is switched off.	**Telefon je isključen.**
I want to ring . . .	**Želim da pozovem...** or **Treba mi...**
What is the code for . . . ?	**Koji je pozivni broj za...?**
What is the international code?	**Koji je izlazni broj (za inostranstvo)?**
The number is . . .	**Broj je...**
The extension is . . .	**Lokal ...**
It's busy.	**Zauzeto je.**
I've been cut off.	**Prekinula mi se veza.**
Where is the nearest public phone?	**Gde je najbliža telefonska govornica?**
digital	**digitalni**
e-mail	**imejl**
fax	**faks**
fax machine	**faks (mašina)**
international operator	**međunarodna centrala**
internet	**internet**
internet cafe	**internet kafe**
landline	**fiksni telefon**
line/connection	**veza**
mobile phone; cell phone	**mobilni (telefon); mobitel**
modem	**modem**
pager	**pejdžer**

COMMUNICATIONS

operator	**centrala**
satellite phone	**satelitski telefon**
sim card	**sim kartica**
Where can I buy a sim card for my mobile phone?	**Gde mogu da kupim sim karticu za moj mobilni?**
to transfer/to put through	**povezati/prebaciti**

Hello . . .
When answering the phone, you say **"molim?"**, **"da!"**, or **"(h)alo?"** If the caller knows you, they will generally respond with **"dobar dan!"**, **"zdravo!"** or **"ćao!"**, prompting your response **"dobar dan!"**, **"zdravo!"** or **"ćao!"**. Now you are ready to start the conversation!

─Faxes & e-mails

Where can I send a fax from?	**Odakle mogu da pošaljem faks?**
I would like to send a fax.	**Želim da pošaljem faks.**
I would like to fax this letter.	**Želim da faksiram ovo pismo.**
Can I fax from here?	**Mogu li da faksiram/ pošaljem faks odavde?**
How much is it to fax?	**Koliko košta slanje faksa?**
Where can I find a place to e-mail from?	**Odakle mogu da pošaljem email?**
Is there an internet café near here?	**Ima li negde ovde internet kafea?**

Can I e-mail from here?	**Mogu li da pošaljem email odavde?**
How much is it to use a computer?	**Koliko košta korišćenje kompjutera?**
How do you turn on this computer?	**Kako se uključuje/ pali ovaj kompjuter?**
The computer has crashed.	**Ovaj kompjuter je krаširao.**
I need help with this computer.	**Treba mi pomoć u vezi sa ovim kompjuterom.**
I don't know how to use this program.	**Ne znam kako se koristi ovaj program.**
I know how to use this program.	**Znam kako se koristi ovaj program.**
I want to print this.	**Želim da odštampam ovo.**

14. THE OFFICE

chair		**stolica**
computer		**kompjuter; računar**
desk		**sto**
drawer		**fioka**
fax		**faks**
file	*paper*	**fascikla**
	computer	**fajl**
laptop		**laptop**
meeting		**sastanak**
paper		**papir**
pen		**olovka**
pencil		**grafitna olovka; drvena olovka**
photocopier		**fotokopir mašina; fotokopirnica**
photocopy		**fotokopija**
printer (computer)		**štampač**
program (computer)		**program**
report		**izveštaj**
ruler		**lenjir**
telephone		**telefon**
telex		**teleks**
typewriter		**pisaća mašina**

15. THE CONFERENCE

article	**članak**
a break (for refreshments)	**pauza**
conference room	**sala za konferenciju; konfereciona sala**
copy	**primerak**
discussion	**diskusija; debata**
forum	**forum**
guest speaker	**gost; gostujući govornik**
a paper	**članak**
podium	**podijum**
projector	**projektor**
session	**sesija; termin**
a session chaired by . . .	**predsedava...**
speaker	**govornik; član**
subject	**predmet; tema**

16. EDUCATION

to add	**sabrati**
addition	**sabiranje; dodatak**
bench	**klupa**
blackboard	**tabla**
book	**knjiga**
calculation	**račun**
to calculate	**računati**
chalk	**kreda**
class	**razred; odeljenje**
to copy	**prepisivati**
to count	**brojati**
crayon	**voštana bojica**
desk	**sto**
difficult	**teško**
to divide	**deliti**
division	**deljenje**
easy	**lako**
eraser	**gumica**
exercise book	**sveska**
to explain	**objasniti**
felt-tip pen	**flomaster**
geography	**geografija**
glue	**lepak**
grammar	**gramatika**
grammar school	**gimnazija**
history	**istorija**
holidays	**raspust**
homework	**domaći (zadatak)**
illiterate	**nepismen**
language	**jezik**
laziness	**lenjost**
to learn by heart	**naučiti napamet**
lesson	**čas**
library	**biblioteka**

c = hi*ts*   č = *ch*urch   ć = *ty*/*chy*   d = *dy*   dž = *j*am

literature	**književnost**
mathematics	**matematika**
memory	**pamćenje**
multiplication	**množenje**
to multiply	**množiti**
notebook	**sveska**
page	**strana; stranica**
paper	**papir**
sheet of paper	**list**
to pass an exam	**položiti ispit**
pen	**(hemijska) olovka**
pencil	**olovka**
progress	**napredak**
to punish	**kazniti**
pupil	**učenik**
to read	**čitati**
to repeat	**ponoviti**
rubber *eraser*	**gumica**
ruler *instrument*	**lenjir**
satchel	**školska torba**
school	**škola**
sheet of paper	**list**
student *university*	**student**
to subtract	**oduzeti**
subtraction	**oduzimanje**
sum	**zbir**
teacher *lower primary school*	**učitelj/učiteljica**
higher primary school	**nastavnik/nastavnica**
high school	**profesor**
to test (academic)	**ispitivanje**
time	**vreme**

Exams . . .

Serbian uses different words for exams and tests depending on the level of education. At school, an oral exam is **odgovaranje**, a written exam is **pismeni zadatak**. At university the general word for both is **ispit**; term-time exams are called **kolokvijum**. A school academic assessment is **kontrolna vežba**, or **pismena vežba**, while homework is **domaći zadatak**, while university assignments are called **seminarski rad**.

h = lo*ch*/*h*it   j = yet   š = *sh*ip   ž = a*z*ure

17. AGRICULTURE

agriculture	**agrikultura; poljoprivreda**
barley	**ječam**
barn	**žitnica; ambar**
cattle	**stoka; marva**
cereals	**žitarice**
combine harvester	**kombajn**
corn	**žito; kukuruz**
cotton	**pamuk**
crops	**žetva; rod**
to cultivate	**gajiti**
earth *land/soil*	**zemlja**
fallowland	**njiva**
farm	**farma (imanje)**
farmer	**poljoprivrednik; zemljoradnik**
farming	**poljoprivreda; zemljoradnja**
(artificial) fertilizer	**(veštačko) đubrivo**
field	**polje; livada; njiva**
fruit	**voće**
furrow	**brazda**
garden	**bašta**
grass	**trava**
to grind	**mleti**
to grow *crops*	**gajiti...**
harvest	**žetva**
hay	**seno**
haystack	**stog sena; plast sena**
irrigation	**navodnjavanje**
leaf	**list**
livestock	**marva**

maize	**kukuruz**
manure	**đubre; gnojivo**
marsh	**močvara**
meadow	**livada**
to milk an animal	**musti**
orchard	**voćnjak**
to pick	**brati**
to plant	**saditi; posaditi**
plow	**plug**
to plow	**orati**
potato	**krompir**
poultry	**živina**
to reap	**žeti**
rice	**pirinač**
root	**koren**
rye	**raž**
season	**godišnje doba**
seeds	**seme**
to shoe a horse	**potkivati konja**
sickle	**srp**
silkworms	**svilene bube**
to sow	**sejati**
spring *of water*	**izvor**
straw	**slama**
tractor	**traktor**
tree	**drvo**
trees	**drveće**
trunk *of tree*	**stablo**
vine	**(vinova) loza**
wheat	**pšenica**
well of water	**bunar**

PLUMS — Among the most important export crops in Serbia and Montenegro are plums — **šljive**. A plum orchard is called a **šljivak**. Plum brandy is called **šljivovica**.

h = lo*ch*/*h*it   j = *y*et   š = *sh*ip   ž = a*z*ure

18. ANIMALS

bat	**slepi miš**
bear	**medved**
boar	**vepar**
bull	**bik**
calf	**tele**
cat	**mačka**
cow	**krava**
deer	**jelen**
dog	**pas**
donkey	**magarac**
ewe	**ovca**
fish	**riba** *(plural* **ribe***)*
flock of sheep	**čopor; stado ovaca**
fox	**lisica**
gazelle	**gazela**
goat	**koza; jarac**
hare	**zec**
herd	**čopor; stado**
hound	**lovački pas**
horse	**konj**
lamb	**jagnje**
lion	**lav**
mare	**kobila**
mole	**krtica**
monkey	**majmun**
mouse	**miš**
mule	**mazga**
ox	**vo**
pig	**svinja**
piglet	**prase**
pony	**poni**
rabbit	**zec**
ram	**ovan**

c = hi**ts**   č = **ch**urch   ć = ty/**chy**   đ = **dy**   dž = **j**am

rat	pacov
sheep	ovca
sheepdog	ovčar
squirrel	veverica
stag	jelen
stallion	pastuv
wolf	vuk

—Birds

bird	ptica
chicken	kokoška; pile
crow	vrana
dove	golubica
duck	patka
eagle	orao
falcon	soko
goose	guska
hawk	soko; jastreb
hen	kokoška
nightingale	slavuj
owl	sova
parrot	papagaj
partridge	jerebica
peacock	paun
pheasant	fazan
pigeon	golub
quail	prepelica
rooster	petao
sparrow	vrabac
swallow	lasta
turkey	ćurka

—Insects & amphibians

ant	mrav
bee	pčela
butterfly	leptir

h = loch/hit   j = yet   š = ship   ž = azure

caterpillar	**gusenica**
cockroach	**buba-švaba**
crab	**rak**
cricket	**zrikavac; cvrčak**
dragonfly	**vilinski konjic**
fish	**riba; ribe**
flea(s)	**buva; buve**
fly	**muva; mušica**
frog	**žaba**
grasshopper	**skakavac**
hedgehog	**jež**
hornet	**stršljen**
insect	**insekt**
lizard	**gušter**
louse	**vaška**
mosquito	**komarac**
scorpion	**škorpija**
snail	**puž**
snake	**zmija**
spider	**pauk**
termite	**termit; beli mrav**
tick	**krlja**
viper	**guja; zmija**
wasp	**osica; zolja**
worm	**crv; glista**

19. COUNTRYSIDE

avalanche	**lavina**
canal	**kanal**
cave	**pećina**
dam	**brana, nasip**
earth	**zemlja**
earthquake	**zemljotres**
fire	**vatra; požar**
flood	**poplava**
footpath	**staza; pešačka staza**
forest	**šuma**
hill	**brdo**
lake	**jezero**
landslide	**lavina**
marsh	**močvara**
mountain	**planina**
mountain pass	**brdski klanac**
mountain range	**planine**
peak	**vrh**
plain	**ravnica; poljana**
plant	**biljka**
pond	**ribnjak**
ravine	**gudura**
river	**reka**
river bank	**(rečna) obala**
rock	**stena**
sand	**pesak**
soil	**tlo; zemlja**
slope	**nagib; strmina**
spring of water	**izvor**
stone	**kamen**
stream	**potok; reka**
summit	**vrh; vrhunac**

COUNTRYSIDE

swamp	**močvara**
tree	**drvo**
valley	**dolina**
waterfall	**vodopad**
a wood	**šuma**

20. WEATHER

> **CLIMATE** — The climate in Serbia and Montenegro ranges from Continental in the north (cold winters and hot, humid summers with well distributed rainfall), to Mediterranean in the central region, to Adriatic along the coast (hot, dry summers and autumns and relatively cold winters with heavy snowfall inland). The temperature rises to at least 30°C in the summer inland, and often falls below zero in the winter months.

What's the weather like?	**Kakvo je vreme?**
The weather is . . . today.	**Danas je ... (vreme).**
cold	**hladno**
cool; fresh	**prohladno; sveže**
cloudy	**oblačno**
foggy	**maglovito**
hot	**toplo**
moderate	**umereno**
misty	**maglovito**
very hot	**vrlo toplo**
very cold	**vrlo hladno**
windy	**vetrovito**

It's going to rain.	**Padaće kiša.**
It is raining.	**Pada kiša.**
It is snowing.	**Pada sneg.**
It's become very cold.	**Dosta je zahladilo.**
It's become warm.	**Otoplilo je.**
It is sunny.	**Sunčano je.**

—Climate words

air	**vazduh**
climate	**klima**
cloud	**oblak**
dew	**rosa**
drought	**suša**

h = lo*ch*/*hit*   j = *y*et   š = *sh*ip   ž = a*z*ure

fog	**magla**
to freeze	**smrzavati; smrznuti**
frost	**mraz**
hail	**grad**
heatwave	**topli talas**
ice	**led; poledica**
lightning	**munja**
mist	**izmaglica**
moon	**mesec**
new moon	**mlad mesec**
full moon	**pun mesec**
rain	**kiša**
rainbow	**duga**
shower of rain	**pljusak**
sky	**nebo**
snow	**sneg**
snowflakes	**pahulje**
star	**zvezda**
stars	**zvezde**
storm	**oluja**
rainstorm	**oluja**
thunderstorm	**grmljavina**
sun	**sunce**
to thaw	**topiti se; otopljavati**
thawed	**otopljen**
thunder	**grom**
weather	**vreme**
weather forecast	**vremenska prognoza**
wind	**vetar**

—Seasons

spring	**proleće**
summer	**leto**
autumn	**jesen**
winter	**zima**

21. CAMPING

Where can we camp?	**Gde možemo da kampujemo?**
Can we camp here?	**Možemo li ovde da kampujemo?**
Is it safe to camp here?	**Je li sigurno ovde za kampovanje?**
Is there drinking water?	**Ima li pitke vode?**
May we light a (camp) fire?	**Smemo li da zapalimo (logorsku) vatru?**

—Equipment

ax	**sekira**
backpack	**ranac**
bucket	**kofa**
campsite	**auto-kamp**
can opener	**otvarač za konzerve**
compass	**kompas; busola**
firewood	**drva za potpalu**
flashlight	**baterijska lampa**
gas canister	**boca plina**
hammer	**čekić**
ice-ax	**nož za led**
icebox	**kutija za led**
lamp	**lampa**
mattress	**dušek**
penknife	**perorez**
rope	**konopac, uže**
sleeping bag	**vreća za spavanje**
stove; camp stove	**rešo**
tent	**šator**
water bottle	**čutura; flaša vode**

22. EMERGENCY

COMPLAINING — If you really feel you have been cheated or misled, raise the matter first with your host or the proprietor of the establishment in question preferably with a smile. Serbians are proud but courteous, with a deeply felt tradition of hospitality, and consider it their duty to help any guest. Angry glares and shouting will get you nowhere.

THEFT — Serbians are law-abiding people, but petty theft does occur. Without undue paranoia, take the usual precautions: watch your wallet or purse, securely lock your equipment and baggage before handing it over to railway or airline porters, and don't leave valuables on display in your hotel room. On buses, look out for pickpockets — keep valuables in front pockets and your bag close to your side. If you are robbed, contact the police. Of course in the more remote areas, sensible precautions should be taken, and always ensure that you go with a guide. In general, follow the same rules as you would in your own country and you will run little risk of encountering crime.

LOST ITEMS — If you lose something, save time and energy by appealing only to senior members of staff or officials. If you have lost items in the street or left anything in public transport, the police may be able to help.

DISABLED ACCESS — The terrain and conditions throughout most of Serbia and Montenegro do not make it easy for any visitor in a wheelchair to get around even at the best of times. Access to most buildings in the cities is difficult, particularly since the majority of lifts function irregularly. Facilities are rarely available in hotels, airports or other public areas. See the vocabulary section at the end of this section for useful expressions and vocabulary.

TOILETS — You will find public utilities located in any important or official building. You may use those in hotels or restaurants. You may sometimes encounter failed plumbing and absence of toilet paper. Occasionally public facilities are attended and a small charge is payable for using the facilities.

Help!	**Upomoć!**
Could you help me, please?	**Pomozite mi molim vas.**
Do you have a telephone?	**Imate li telefon?**
Where is the nearest telephone?	**Gde je najbliži telefon?**

c = hi*ts*   č = *ch*urch   ć = *ty/chy*   đ = *dy*   dž = *j*am

Does the phone work?	**Jel' radi telefon?**
Get help quickly!	**Pomoć, brzo!**
Call the police.	**Zovite policiju.**
I'll call the police.	**Pozvaću policiju.**
Is there a doctor near here?	**Ima li lekera negde ovde?**
Call a doctor.	**Zovite doktora.**
Call an ambulance.	**Zovite hitnu pomoć.**
I'll get medical help!	**Pozvaću lekara.**
Where is the doctor?	**Gde je doctor?**
Is there a doctor?	**Ima li lekara?**
Where is the hospital?	**Gde je bolnica?**
Where is the pharmacy?	**Gde je apoteka?**
Where is the dentist?	**Gde je zubar?**
Where is the police station?	**Gde je policijska stanica?**
Take me to a doctor.	**Vodite me kod lekara.**
There's been an accident.	**Desila se nesreća.**
Is anyone hurt?	**Je li iko povređen? Ima i povređenih?**
This man is hurt.	**Ovaj gospodin je povređen.**
This woman is hurt.	**Ova gospođa je povređena.**
This child is hurt.	**Ovo dete je povredno.**
There are people injured.	**Ima povređenih.**
Don't move!	**Ne pomerajte se!**
Go away!	**Idite!; Odlazite!**
Stand back!	**Sklonite se!**

I am lost.	*m*	**Izgubio sam se.**
	f	**Izgubila sam se.**
I am ill.	*m*	**Bolestan sam.**
	f	**Bolesna sam.**
I've been robbed.		**Opljačkan/-a sam.**

Stop, thief!	**Lopov!**
My . . . has been stolen.	**Ukraden/-a/-o mi je...**
I have lost . . .	**Izgubio/-la sam...**
my bags	**prtljag**
my camera equipment	**foto-aparat; kameru**
my handbag	**tašnu**
my laptop computer	**leptop**
my money	**novac**
my passport	**pasoš**
my sound equipment	**zvučnu opremu**
my traveler's checks	**putne čekove**
my wallet	**novčanik**
My possessions are insured.	**Osiguran/-a sam.**
I have a problem.	**Imam problem.**
I didn't do it.	**Nisam ja to uradio.**
I'm sorry.	**Izvinite.; Žao mi je.**
I apologize.	**Izvinjavam se.**
I didn't realise ...	**Nisam znao/znala...**
I want to contact my embassy.	**Želim da kontaktiram moju ambasadu.**
I speak English.	**Ja govorim engleski.**
I need an interpreter.	**Treba mi tumač.**
Where are the toilets?	**Gde je toalet.**

—Disabilities

wheelchair	**kolica**
disabled	**invalid**
Do you have seats for the disabled?	**Imate li sedišta za invalide?**
Do you have access for the disabled?	**Imate li prilaz za invalidska kolica?**
Do you have facilities for the disabled?	**Imate li uslove za invalide?**

c = hi*ts*   č = *ch*urch   ć = *ty/chy*   d = *dy*   dž = *j*am

23. HEALTHCARE

> **INSURANCE** — Make sure any insurance policy you take out covers Serbia, although this will only help in flying you out in case of a serious accident or illness. Consult your doctor for any shots required or recommended when making any trip outside of North America and Western Europe. Yugoslavia has an international medical agreement which means that foreigners are entitled to medical care. As of recently, however, most domestic patients have had to pay for examination, services, medication and anesthetics. Overall, medical care in Serbia and Montenegro is often very good and you are unlikely to leave the doctor without due attention or prescription. There are no diseases in Yugoslavia which require immunization or vaccination. All you might need is a mosquito repellant in summer.

What's the trouble?		**U čemu je problem?**
I am sick.	*m*	**Bolestan sam.**
	f	**Bolesna sam.**
My companion is sick.	*m*	**Moj saputnik je bolestan.**
	f	**Moja saputnica je bolesna.**
May I see a female doctor?		**Mogu li dobiti doktorku/ ženskog lekara?**
I have medical insurance.		**Imam zdravstveno osiguranje.**
Please take off your shirt.		**Molim vas skinite košulju/ skinite se.**
Please take off your clothes.		**Molim vas skinite se.**
How long have you had this problem?		**Koliko dugo patite od ovog problema?**
How long have you been feeling sick?		**Koliko dugo se osećate loše?**
Where does it hurt?		**Gde vas boli?**
It hurts here.		**Boli me ovde.**

h = lo*ch*/*h*it   j = yet   š = *sh*ip   ž = a*z*ure

I have been vomiting. *m*	**Povraćao sam.**
f	**Povraćala sam.**
I feel dizzy.	**Vrti mi se u glavi.**
I can't eat.	**Ne mogu da jedem.**
I can't sleep.	**Ne mogu da spavam.**
I feel worse.	**Osećam se još gore.**
I feel better.	**Bolje mi je.**
Do you have diabetes?	**Patite li od diabetesa/ šećerne bolesti?**
Do you have epilepsy?	**Imate li epilepsiju.**
Do you have asthma?	**Imate li astmu?**
I'm pregnant.	**Trudna sam.**
I have . . .	**Imam...**
You have . . . *formal*	**Imate...**
informal	**Imaš...**
pains.	**bolove.**
a temperature.	**temperaturu.**
an allergy.	**alergiju.**
an infection.	**infekciju.**
an itch.	**svrab.**
a rash.	**osip na koži.**
constipation.	**zatvor.**
diarrhea.	**proliv.**
fever.	**groznicu.**
hepatitis.	**hepatitis.**
indigestion.	**probleme sa varenjem.**
influenza.	**grip.**
a heart condition.	**problem sa srcem.**
a fracture	**prelom.**
I have a cold.	**Imam prehladu.** *or* **Prehlađen,-a sam.**
You have a cold. *formal*	**Imate prehladu.** *or* **Prehlađeni ste.**

informal	**Imaš prehladu.** or **Prehlađen,-a si.**
I have a cough.	**Imam kašalj.**
You have a cough. *formal*	**Imate kašalj.**
informal	**Imaš kašalj.**
I have a headache.	**Boli me glava.** or **Imam glavobolju.**
You have a headache. *formal*	**Boli vas glava.** or **Imate glavobolju.**
informal	**Boli te glava.** or **Imaš glavobolju.**
I have a sore throat.	**Boli me grlo.**
I have backache.	**Bole me leđa.**
I have pins and needles... in my leg.	**Utrnula mi je... noga.**
I have stomachache.	**Boli me stomak.**
I have toothache.	**Boli me zub.**
I take this medication.	**Pijem ovaj lek.**
I need medication for . . .	**Treba mi lek za...**
What type of medication is this?	**Kakav je ovo lek?**
What pills are these?	**Koje su ovo pilule/ tablete?**
How many times a day must I take this medicine?	**Koliko puta dnevno treba da pijem ovaj lek?**
When should I stop?	**Kada treba da prestanem?**
I'm on antibiotics.	**Pijem antibiotike.**
I'm allergic to antibiotics.	**Alergičan/alergična sam na antibiotike.**
I'm allergic to penicillin.	**Alergičan/alergičina sam na pencilin.**
I have been vaccinated.	**Primio/primila sam vakcinu.**
I have my own syringe.	**Imam svoj špric.**

h = lo*ch*/hit   j = yet   š = *sh*ip   ž = a*z*ure

Is it possible for me to travel?   **Smem li da putujem?**

—Health words

AIDS	**sida**
alcoholism	**alkoholizam**
to amputate	**amputirati**
anemia	**anemija**
anesthetic	**anestezija**
anesthetist	**anestetičar**
antibiotic	**antibiotik**
antiseptic	**antiseptik**
appetite	**apetit**
artery	**arterija**
artificial arm	**veštačka ruka; proteza**
artificial eye	**vestačko oko**
artificial leg	**vestačka noga; proteza; štula**
aspirin	**aspirin**
bandage medical	**zavoj**
Band-Aid *plaster*	**hanzaplast**
bladder	**bešika**
blood	**krv**
blood group	**krvna grupa**
blood pressure	**krvni pritisak**
high blood pressure	**visok pritisak**
low blood pressure	**nizak pritisak**
blood transfusion	**transfuzija**
bone	**kost**
brain	**mozak**
bug insect	**insekt**
burn medical	**opekotina**
cancer	**rak**
catheter	**kateter**
cholera	**kolera**
clinic	**klinika**

c = hi*ts*   č = *ch*urch   ć = *ty/chy*   d = *dy*   dž = *j*am

cold *medical*	**prehlada**
constipated: Are you constipated?	**Imate li zatvor?**
cotton wool	**vata**
cough	**kašalj**
cream *ointment*	**melem; krema; mast za rane**
to dehydrate	**dehidrirati**
dentist	**zubar**
diarrhea	**proliv**
diet	**dijet**
dressing *medical*	**zavoj za rane**
drug *medical*	**lek**
drug *narcotic*	**droga**
dysentery	**dizenterija**
ear	**uho**
ears	**uši**
ear drum	**bubna opna**
epidemic	**epidemija**
eye	**oko**
eyes	**oči**
fever	**groznica**
flea	**buva**
flu	**grip**
frostbite	**promrzlost**
gall bladder	**žuč**
gently!	**polako!**
germs	**bakterije**
gut	**utroba**
guts	**creva**
hand: left hand	**leva ruka**
right hand	**desna ruka**
hard! *vigorously*	**brzo!**
health	**zdravlje**
heart attack	**srčani napad; infarkt**
heel	**peta**

h = lo*ch*/*h*it   j = *y*et   š = *sh*ip   ž = a*z*ure

hip	**kuk**
hips	**kukovi**
hygiene	**higijena**
infant	**beba**
infected	**inficiran; zaražen**
infection	**infekcija; zaraza**
intestine(s)	**utroba; creva**
joint	**zglob**
kidney	**bubreg**
kidneys	**bubrezi**
lice	**vaške**
limbs	**udovi**
maternity hospital	**porodilište**
milk *mother's*	**mleko; majčino mleko**
cow's	**kravlje mleko**
goat's	**kozje mleko**
powdered	**mleko u prahu**
mouth	**usta**
muscle	**mišić**
navel	**pupak**
needle	**igla**
nerve	**nerv; živac**
newborn child	**novorođenče**
nose	**nos**
nurse	**medicinska sestra**
ointment *cream*	**mast za rane; krema; melem**
operating theater	**operaciona sala**
(surgical) operation	**(hirurška) operacija**
organ (of body)	**(telesni) organ**
oxygen	**kiseonik**
painkiller	**anelgetik; tableta protiv bolova**
palm of hand	**dlan**
pancreas	**pankreas**

c = hi**ts**   č = **ch**urch   ć = t**y/chy**   đ = **dy**   dž = **j**am

physiotherapy	**fizioterapija**
placenta	**posteljica**
plaster *medical*	**hanzaplast; flaster**
plaster cast *medical*	**gips**
pupil of eye	**zenica**
rabies	**besnilo**
rash on skin	**osip na koži**
rib	**rebro**
ribs	**rebra**
rib cage	**grudni koš**
saliva	**pljuvačka**
shoulder blade	**(ramena) lopatica**
shrapnel	**šrapnel**
side of body	**strana tela**
skin	**koža**
skull	**lobanja**
sleeping pill	**tableta za spavanje**
snakebite	**ujed zmije**
sole of foot	**taban**
spinal column; spine	**kičma**
spinal cord	**kičmena moždina**
stethoscope	**stetoskop**
stump *of limb*	**patrljak**
surgeon	**hirurg**
(act of) surgery	**hirurška operacija**
syringe	**špric**
syrup *medical*	**sirup**
thermometer	**termometar; toplomer**
thigh	**butina**
throat	**grlo**
to vomit	**povraćati**
tooth	**zub**
teeth	**zubi**
torture	**mučenje; tortura**
trachea	**dušnik**
tranquilizer	**tableta za smirenje**

HEALTHCARE

tuberculosis	**tuberkuloza**
umbilical cord	**pupčana vrpca**
urine	**urin; mokraća**
vein	**vena**
vertebra	**pršljen**
vitamins	**vitamini**
waist	**struk**
windpipe	**dušnik**

—Eyecare

I have broken my glasses.	**Polomio/Polomila sam naočare.**
Can you repair them?	**Možete li da ih popravite.**
I need new lenses.	**Trebaju mi nova sočiva.**
When will they be ready?	**Kada će biti gotovo?**
How much do I owe you?	**Koliko košta?**
contact lenses	**sočiva**
contact lens solution	**rastvor/tečnost za sočiva**

24. RELIEF AID

Can you help me?	**Možete li da mi pomognete?**
Can you speak English?	**Govorite li engleski?**
Who is in charge?	**Ko je odgovoran?**
Fetch the main person in charge.	**Pozovite mi upravnika/ šefa.**
What's the name of this town?	**Kako se zove ovaj grad?**
How many people live there?	**Koliko ima stanovnika?**
What's the name of that river?	**Kako se zove ta reka?**
How deep is it?	**Koliko je duboka?**
Is the bridge down?	**Je li most spušten?**
Is the bridge still standing?	**Da li još uvek stoji taj most?**
Where can we ford the river?	**Gde možemo da pređemo reku?**
What is the name of that mountain?	**Kako se zove ta planina?**
How high is it?	**Koliko je visoka?**
Where is the border?	**Gde je granica?**
Is it safe?	**Je li sigurno/bezbedno?**
Show me.	**Pokažite mi.**
Is there anyone trapped?	**Je li neko zaglavljen/ u zamci?**
Is the building safe?	**Je li zgrada bezbedna?**
It's going to collapse!	**Ruši se!**

h = loch/hit   j = yet   š = ship   ž = azure

Get out (of the building) now!	**Odmah izađite (iz zgrade)!**
Can you hear any sound?	**Da li čujete nešto?**
Silence!	**Tišina!**

—Checkpoints

checkpoint	**rampa, prelaz**
roadblock	**barikada**
Stop!	**Stop!; Stoj!**
Do not move!	**Ne mrdaj!**
Go!	**Napred!**
Who's there?	**Ko je?**
Who are you?	**Ko ste vi?**
Don't shoot!	**Ne pucaj!**
Help!	**Upomoć!**
Help me!	**Pomozite mi!**
no entry/access	**zabranjen ulaz/prilaz**
emergency exit	**izlaz u nuždi**
straight on	**pravo, napred**
turn left	**skrenite levo**
turn right	**skrenite desno**
this way	**ovamo, ovuda**
that way	**tamo**
Keep quiet!	**Tišina!**
You are right.	**U pravu ste.**
You are wrong.	**Niste u pravu.**
I am ready.	**Spreman/spremna sam.**
I am in a hurry.	**Žurim.**
What's that?	**Šta je to?**
Come in!	**Slobodno!; Uđite!**
That's all!	**To je sve!**

—Food distribution

feeding station	**kantina**
How many people are in your family?	**Koliko članova porodice imate?**

c = hits   č = church   ć = ty/chy   đ = dy   dž = jam

How many children?	**Koliko dece?**
You must come back . . .	**Morate da se vratite...**
this afternoon	**popodne**
tonight	**večeras**
tomorrow	**sutra**
the day after tomorrow	**preksutra**
next week	**sledeće nedelje**

Here is water for you.	**Ovo je voda za vas.**
Here is grain for you.	**Ovo je žito za vas.**
Here is food for you.	**Ovo je hrana za vas.**
Here is fuel for you.	**Ovo je gorivo za vas.**
Please form a queue (here/there)!	**Molim vas stanite u red (ovde/tamo)!**

—Road repair

Is the road passable?	**Je li put otvoren?**
Is the road blocked?	**Je li put blokiran?**

We are repairing the road.	**Popravljamo put.**
We are repairing the bridge.	**Popravljamo most.**
We need . . .	**Trebaju nam...**
wood	**drva**
We need . . .	**Treba nam...**
a rock	**kamen**
rocks	**kamenje**
gravel	**šljunak**
sand	**pesak**
fuel	**gorivo**

Lift!	**Diži!**
Drop it!	**Spuštaj!**
Now!	**Sad!**
All together!	**Svi zajedno!**

h = lo*ch*/*h*it   j = *y*et   š = *sh*ip   ž = a*z*ure

RELIEF AID

—Mines

mine *noun*	**mina**
mines	**mine**
minefield	**minsko polje**
to lay mines	**postavljati mine**
to hit a mine	**naići na minu**
to clear a mine	**čistiti mine**
mine detector	**minolovac; minodetektor**
mine disposal	**dezaktiviranje mina**

Are there any mines near here?	**Ima li mina ovde?**
What type are they?	**Koje su vrste?**
anti-vehicle	**protiv vozila**
anti-personnel	**protivpešadijska**
plastic	**plastične**
magnetic	**magnetske**
What size are they?	**Koje su veličine?**
What color are they?	**Koje su boje?**
Are they marked?	**Jesu li obeležene?**
How?	**Kako?**
How many mines are there?	**Koliko ima mina?**
When were they laid?	**Kada su postavljene?**
Can you take me to the minefields?	**Možete li me odvesti do minskog polja?**
Are there any booby traps near there?	**Ima li nekih nagaznih mina ovde?**
Are they made from	**Da li se sastoje od**
grenades,	**granata**
high explosives,	**eksploziva**
or something else?	**ili nečeg drugog?**

Are they in a building?	**Da li se nalaze u zgradi?**
on paths?	**na stazama?**
on roads?	**na putevima?**

on bridges?	na mostovima?
or elsewhere?	ili negde drugde?
Can you show me?	Možete li da mi pokažete?
Don't go near that!	Ne prilazi!
Don't touch that!	Ne diraj!

—Other words

airforce	avijacija
ambulance	ambulanta
armored car	blindirana kola
army	armija, vojska
artillery	artiljerija
barbed wire	bodljikava žica
bomb	bomba
bomber	bombarder
bomblet	bombica
bullet	metak
cannon	top
cluster bomb	rasprskavajuća bomba
disaster	nesreća
drought	suša
earthquake	zemljotres
famine	glad
fighter *plane*	lovački avion
gun *pistol*	pištolj
rifle	puška
cannon	top
machinegun	mašinka
missile	raketa
missiles	rakete
mortar *weapon*	minobacač
natural disaster	prirodna nepogoda
navy	mornarica
nuclear power	nuklearna energija

h = lo*ch*/*h*it   j = yet   š = *sh*ip   ž = a*z*ure

nuclear power station	**nuklearna elektrana**
officer	**oficir; zvanično lice**
parachute	**padobranac**
peace	**mir**
people	**narod; ljudi**
pistol	**pištolj**
refugee camp	**izbeglički logor**
refugee	**izbeglica**
refugees	**izbeglice**
relief aid	**humanitarna pomoć**
sack	**džak**
shell	**granata**
shelter	**skrovište**
tank	**tenk**
troops	**trupe**
unexploded ammunition	**ne eksplodirana municija**
unexploded bomb	**ne eksplodirana bomba**
unexploded mine	**ne eksplodirana mina**
war	**rat**
weapon	**oružje**

25. TOOLS

binoculars	**dvogled**
brick	**cigla**
brush	**četka**
cable	**kabl**
cooker	**šporet**
mobile cooker	**rešo**
crane	**dizalica**
crowbar	**metalna poluga; pajser**
drill	**bušilica**
gas bottle/canister	**boca za plin**
hammer	**čekić**
handle	**ručka**
hose	**crevo**
insecticide	**insekticid**
ladder	**merdevine**
machine	**mašina**
nail	**ekser**
padlock	**katanac**
paint	**farba, boja**
pickaxe	**trnokop**
plank	**daska**
plastic	**plastika**
rope	**konopac; uže**
rubber	**guma**
rust	**rđa**
saw	**testera**
scissors	**makaze**
screw	**šraf**
screwdriver	**šrafciger**
spade	**lopata**
spanner/wrench	**izvijač; natezač**
string	**žica**
telescope	**teleskop**
varnish	**lak**
wire	**žica**

h = lo*ch*/*h*it   **j** = *y*et   **š** = *sh*ip   **ž** = a*z*ure

26. THE CAR

Where can I rent a car?	**Gde mogu da iznajmim auto?**
Where can I rent a car with a driver?	**Gde mogu da iznajmim auto sa šoferom?**
How much is it per day?	**Koliko košta dnevno?**
How much is it per week?	**Koliko košta nedeljno?**
Can I park here?	**Mogu li ovde da parkiram?**
Are we on the right road for. . . ?	**Je li ovo put za...?**
Where is the nearest filling station?	**Gde je najbliža benzinska pumpa?**
Fill the tank please.	**Napunite mi rezervoar, molim vas.**
normal/diesel	**normalno/dizel gorivo**
Check the oil/tires/ battery, please.	**Molim vas proverite mi ulje/gume/akumulator.**

—Emergencies

I've broken down.	**Stala su mi kola.** or **Pokvarila su mi se kola.** or **Imam kvar.**
I have a puncture.	**Pukla mi je guma.**
I have run out of gas.	**Nestalo mi benzina.**
Our car is stuck.	**Zaglavila su mi se kola.**
There's something wrong with my car.	**Imam problem sa kolima.**
We need a mechanic.	**Treba nam auto mehaničar.**

c = hits   č = church   ć = ty/chy   đ = dy   dž = jam

Where is the nearest garage?	Gde je najbliža benzinska pumpa/ servisna stanica.
Can you tow us?	Možete li da nas vučete?
Can you jumpstart the car (by pushing)?	Možete li da nas pogurate?
There's been an accident.	Desila se (saobraćajna) nesreća.
My car has been stolen.	Ukrali su mi kola/ auto.
Call the police.	Zovite policiju.
The tire is flat.	Isupstila mi je guma.

—Car words

driving license	vozačka dozvola
insurance policy	osiguranje
car papers	vozačke isprave
car registration/numberplate	registracija
accelerator	pedala za gas
air	vazduh
anti-freeze	antifriz
battery	akumulator
bonnet/hood	poklopac
boot/trunk	gepek
brake	kočnica
bumper	branik
car park	parking
clutch	kvačilo
driver	vozač
engine	motor
exhaust	auspuh
fan belt	kaiš ventilatora
gear	brzina
gear-box	menjač

h = loch/hit   j = yet   š = ship   ž = azure

indicator light	**žmigavac**
inner tube	**unutrašnja guma**
jack	**dizalica**
mechanic	**auto-mehaničar**
neutral drive	**ler**
oil	**ulje**
oilcan	**kanta sa uljem**
passenger	**putnik**
petrol	**benzin**
radiator	**radijator**
reverse	**rikverc**
seat	**sedište**
spare tyre/tire	**pomoćna guma**
speed	**brzina**
steering wheel	**volan**
tank	**rezervoar**
tyre/tire	**guma**
windshield wipers	**brisači**
windscreen/windshield	**šoferšajbna**

27. SPORTS

Sports culture is traditionally very well developed in Serbia and Montenegro. Favourite sports include ball games such as soccer, basketball, handball, and volleyball as well as tennis and skiing. Most schoolyards, for example, have open-air soccer and basketball courts, and every major town has a well-equipped sports center with indoors and/or open-air swimming pools and tennis fields. Professional sports teams have also distinguished themselves internationally mainly in basketball (Yugoslavia won two consecutive world championships), volleyball, water polo, and soccer. The most famous Yugoslav soccer teams include Red Star Belgrade and Partizan Belgrade. Tennis stars originating from Yugoslavia include Monica Seleš and Jelena Dokić.

athletics	**atletika**
ball	**lopta**
basketball	**košarka; basket**
chess	**šah**
goal	**gol; go**
handball	**rukomet**
horse racing	**konjske trke**
horseback riding	**jahanje**
match	**utakmica**
soccer match	**futbalska utakmica**
pitch	**teren**
referee	**sudija**
rugby	**ragbi**
skiing	**skijanje**
soccer	**futbal; fudbal**
stadium	**stadion**
swimming	**plivanje**
team	**ekipa; tim**
volleyball	**odbojka**
water polo	**vaterpolo**
wrestling	**rvanje**

h = lo*ch*/*h*it   j = *y*et   š = *sh*ip   ž = a*z*ure

Who won?	**Ko je pobedio?**
What's the score?	**Koji je rezultat?**
a draw	**Nerešeno**
Who scored?	**Ko je dao go?**

Weights & measures . . .

Serbia and Montenegro use the metric system. Traditional "yeast-pieces" used to be made and sold in pounds but all other groceries are sold in metric. Here is a list of international units — for reference purposes, translations are included for the most common imperial units:

kilometer	**kilometar**
meter	**metar**
mile	**milja**
foot	**stopa**
yard	**jarda**
acre	**jutro; aker**
hectare	**hektar**
gallon	**galon**
liter	**litar**
kilogram	**kilogram**
ton; tonne	**tona**
gram	**gram**
pound	**funta**

28. THE BODY

ankle	**članak na nozi**
arm	**ruka**
back	**leđa**
beard	**brada**
blood	**krv**
body	**telo**
bone	**kost**
bottom	**tur; zadnjica**
breast	**grud; dojka**
chest	**grudi**
calf *leg*	**list**
cheek(s)	**obraz(i)**
chin	**brada**
ear	**uho; uvo**
elbow	**lakat**
eye	**oko**
eyebrow	**obrva**
eyelashes	**trepavice**
face	**lice**
finger	**prst**
fingers	**prsti**
fist	**šaka**
foot	**stopalo**
feet	**stopala**
genitals	**genitalije; polni organi**
hair	**kosa**
a hair	**dlaka**
hand	**ruka**
head	**glava**
heart	**srce**
index finger	**kažiprst**
jaw	**vilica**
kidney	**bubreg**

h = lo*ch*/*h*it   j = yet   š = ship   ž = azure

knee	**koleno**
leg	**noga**
lip	**usna**
liver	**jetra**
lung(s)	**plućno krilo;**
	pluća
mustache	**brkovi**
mouth	**usta**
nail of finger/toe	**nokat**
navel	**pupak**
neck	**vrat**
nose	**nos**
rib	**rebro**
ribs	**rebra**
shoulder	**rame**
skin	**koža**
stomach	**stomak**
throat	**grlo**
thumb	**palac**
toe	**nožni prst**
tongue	**jezik**
tooth	**zub**
teeth	**zubi**
womb	**materica**
wrist	**(ručni) zglob**

29. POLITICS

aid worker		**humanitarni radnik**
ambassador		**ambasador**
to arrest		**uhapsiti**
assassination		**atentat**
assembly:	meeting	**skupština**
	parliament	**parlament; skupština**
autonomy		**nezavisnost; autonomija**
cabinet		**kabinet**
a charity		**dobrovoljna organizacija**
citizen		**građanin**
civil rights		**građanska prava**
civil war		**građanski rat**
coalition		**koalicija**
condemn		**osuditi**
constitution		**ustav**
convoy		**konvoj**
corruption		**korupcija**
coup d'etat		**puč**
crime		**kriminal; kriminalno delo; prekršaj**
criminal	*person*	**kriminalac**
	adjective	**kriminalan**
crisis		**kriza**
dictator		**diktator**
debt		**dug**
democracy		**demokratija**
dictatorship		**diktatura**
diplomatic ties		**diplomatske veze**
displaced person		**iseljeno lice; raseljeno lice**
displaced persons/people		**raseljena lica**
election		**izbor**
embassy		**ambasada**

ethnic cleansing	**etničko čišćenje**
exile	**izgnanstvo; prognanstvo; egzil**
free	**slobodan**
freedom	**sloboda**
government	**vlada**
guerrilla	**gerila; neredovna vojska**
hostage	**taoc**
humanitarian aid	**humanitarna pomoć**
human rights	**ljudska prava**
imam	**imam**
independence	**nezavisnost; samostalnost**
independent	**nezavisan (nezavisna/ nezavisno)**
independent state	**nezavisna država**
judge	**sudija**
killer	**ubica**
king	**kralj**
law court	**sud**
law	**zakon**
lawyer	**advokat**
leader	**vođa**
left-wing	**levica**
liberation	**oslobođenje**
majority	**većina**
mercenary	**najamnik; plaćeni ubica**
minister	**ministar**
ministry	**ministartsvo**
minority	**manjina**
ethnic minority	**etnička manjina**
minority vote	**glas manjine**
murder	**ubistvo**
opposition	**opozicija**
parliament	**parlament; skupština**

upper house	**gornji dom**
lower house	**donji dom**
(political) party	**politička stranka**
politics	**politika**
peace	**mir**
peacekeeping troops	**mirovne trupe**
politician	**političar**
president	**predsednik**
prime minister	**premijer**
prison	**zatvor**
prisoner-of-war	**ratni zarobljenik**
POW camp	**zarobljenički logor**
protest	**protest**
reactionary *adjective*	**reakcionaran**
	(reakcionarna/-o)
Red Cross	**Crveni krst**
refugee	**izbeglica**
refugees	**izbeglice**
revolution	**revolucija**
right-wing	**desnica**
robbery	**pljačka**
seat (in assembly)	**poslaničko mesto**
secret police	**tajna služba**
socialism	**socijalizam**
socialist	**socijalistički**
spy	**špijun**
struggle	**borba**
to testify	**svedočiti**
theft	**krađa**
trade union	**radničko udruženje**
treasury	**državna blagajna**
United Nations	**Ujedinjene Nacije**
veto	**veto**
vote	**glas**
vote-rigging	**nameštanje izbora**
voting	**glasanje**

30. WAR

airplane	**avion**
air-raid	**vazdušni napad**
ambush	**zaseda**
ammunition	**municija**
anti-aircraft gun	**protiv-vazdušna artiljerija**
armored car	**blindirana kola**
arms	**oružje**
army	**vojska; armija**
artillery	**artiljerija**
assault; attack	**napad**
aviation	**avijacija**
bayonet	**bajonet**
to beat, overcome	**prevazići**
bomb	**bomba**
bombardment	**bombardovanje**
butt of rifle	**kundak**
to camouflage	**zamaskirati**
captain	**kapetan**
cartridge	**metak; naboj; šaržer**
ceasefire	**primirje**
chief of staff	**komandujući**
to command	**komandovati**
to conquer	**osvojiti**
dagger	**bodež; kama**
defeat	**poraz**
to defeat	**poraziti**
to destroy	**uništiti**
detonation	**detonacija**
enemy	**neprijatelj**
to evacuate	**evakuisati**
to explode	**eksplodirati**
to free	**osloboditi**

c = hits   č = church   ć = ty/chy   d = dy   dž = jam

freedom	**sloboda**
general	**general**
grenade	**granata**
gun	**puška**
gun barrel	**burence**
helicopter	**helikopter**
hostage	**taoc**
to invade	**napasti**
invasion	**upad**
to kill	**ubiti**
to liberate	**osloboditi**
liberty	**sloboda**
to loot	**pljačkati**
to lose	**izgubiti**
machine gun	**mašinka**
martyr	**mučenik**
military university	**vojna akademija**
military school	**vojna akademija**
mine	**mina**
anti-personnel mine	**protivpešadijska mina**
anti-tank mine	**protivoklopna mina**
munitions	**municija**
opponent	**protivnik**
patrol	**patrola**
peace	**mir**
to make peace	**potpisati mirovni ugovor**
personnel *military*	**vojska**
pilot	**pilot**
pistol	**pištolj**
plane	**avion**
prisoner	**zatvorenik; zarobljenik**
to take prisoner	**zarobiti**
to pursue	**progoniti; pratiti**
raid	**napad**
air-raid	**vazdušni napad**
regiment	**puk**

reinforcements	**pojačanje**
to resist	**odoleti**
to retreat	**povlačiti se; povući se**
rifle	**puška**
rocket	**raketa**
shell *military*	**granata**
shelter	**skrovište**
to shoot down	**oboriti**
shrapnel	**šrapnel**
siege	**opsada**
soldier	**vojnik**
spy	**špijun**
staff army	**vojno osoblje**
submachine gun	**mitraljez**
to surrender	**predati se**
to surround	**opkoliti**
to take shelter	**sakriti se**
tank	**tenk**
target	**meta**
truce	**primirje**
victory	**pobeda**
war	**rat**
weapon	**oružje**
to win	**pobediti**
to wound	**raniti**

31. TIME

century	**vek; stoleće**
decade	**decenija**
year	**godina**
month	**mesec**
week	**nedelja**
day	**dan**
hour	**sat**
minute	**minut**
second	**sekunda**
dawn	**zora**
sunrise	**izlazak sunca**
morning	**jutro**
daytime	**dan**
noon	**podne**
afternoon	**popodne**
evening	**veče**
sunset	**zalazak sunca**
night	**noć**
midnight	**ponoć**
three days before	**pre tri dana**
the day before yesterday	**prekjuče**
yesterday	**juče**
today	**danas**
tomorrow	**sutra**
the day after tomorrow	**preksutra**
three days from now	**za tri dana**
the year before last	**pretprošla godina**
last year	**prošla godina**
this year	**ova godina**
next year	**sledeća godina**
the year after next	**za dve godine**

h = lo*ch*/*h*it   j = *y*et   š = *sh*ip   ž = a*z*ure

last week	**prošla nedelja**
this week	**ova nedelja**
next week	**sledeća nedelja**
last night	**sinoć**
this morning	**jutros**
just now	**upravo, sad**
now	**sada**
this afternoon	**popodne**
this evening	**večeras**
tonight	**noćas**
yesterday morning	**juče ujutro**
yesterday afternoon	**juče popodne**
yesterday night	**sinoć**
tomorrow morning	**sutra ujutro**
tomorrow afternoon	**sutra popodne**
tomorrow night	**sutra uveče**
in the morning	**ujutro**
in the afternoon	**popodne**
in the evening	**uveče**
past	**prošlost**
present	**sadašnjost**
future	**budućnost**
What day is it today?	**Koji je dan danas?**
What date is it today?	**Koji je danas datum?**
What time is it?	**Kol'ko ima sati?**
It is . . . o'clock.	**...sati i ...minuta**

—Seasons

summer	**leto**
autumn	**jesen**
winter	**zima**
spring	**proleće**

—Days of the week

Monday	**ponedeljak**
Tuesday	**utorak**
Wednesday	**sreda**
Thursday	**četvrtak**
Friday	**petak**
Saturday	**subota**
Sunday	**nedelja**

—Months

January	**januar**
February	**februar**
March	**mart**
April	**april**
May	**maj**
June	**jun**
July	**jul**
August	**avgust**
September	**septembar**
October	**oktobar**
November	**novembar**
December	**decembar**

—Star signs

Aries	**Ovan**
Taurus	**Bik**
Gemini	**Blizanci**
Cancer	**Rak**
Leo	**Lav**
Virgo	**Devica**
Libra	**Vaga**
Scorpio	**Škorpija**
Sagittarius	**Strelac**
Capricorn	**Jarac**
Aquarius	**Vodolija**
Pisces	**Ribe**

h = lo*ch*/*h*it   j = *y*et   š = *sh*ip   ž = a*z*ure

32. NUMBERS

0	nula		
1	jedan	31	trideset jedan
2	dva	32	trideset dva
3	tri	33	trideset tri
4	četiri; četri	34	trideset četiri
5	pet	35	trideset pet
6	šest	36	trideset šest
7	sedam	37	trideset sedam
8	osam	38	trideset osam
9	devet	39	trideset devet
10	deset	40	četrdeset
11	jedean(a)est	41	četrdeset jedan
12	dvan(a)est	42	četrdeset dva
13	trin(a)est	43	četrdeset tri
14	četrn(a)est	44	četrdeset četiri
15	petn(a)est	45	četrdeset pet
16	šesn(a)est	46	četrdeset šest
17	sedamn(a)est	47	četrdeset sedam
18	osamn(a)est	48	četrdeset osam
19	devetn(a)est	49	četrdeset devet
20	dvadeset	50	pedeset
21	dvedeset jedan	51	pedeset jedan
22	dvadeset dva	52	pedeset dva
23	dvadeset tri	53	pedeset tri
24	dvadeset četiri	54	pedeset četiri
25	dvadeset pet	55	pedeset pet
26	dvadeset šest	56	pedeset šest
27	dvadeset sedam	57	pedeset sedam
28	dvadeset osam	58	pedeset osam
29	dvadeset devet	59	pedeset devet
30	trideset	60	šezdeset

c = hi*ts*   č = *ch*urch   ć = *ty/chy*   đ = *dy*   dž = *j*am

61	šezdeset jedan	81	osamdeset jedan
62	šezdeset dva	82	osamdeset dva
63	šezdeset tri	83	osamdeset tri
64	šezdeset četiri	84	osamdeset četiri
65	šezdeset pet	85	osamdeset pet
66	šezdeset šest	86	osamdeset šest
67	šezdeset sedam	87	osamdeset sedam
68	šezdeset osam	88	osamdeset osam
69	šezdeset devet	89	osamdeset devet
70	sedamdeset	90	devedeset
71	sedamdeset jedan	91	devedeset jedan
72	sedamdeset dva	92	devedeset dva
73	sedamdeset tri	93	devedeset tri
74	sedamdeset četiri	94	devedeset četiri
75	sedamdeset pet	95	devedeset pet
76	sedamdeset šest	96	devedeset šest
77	sedamdeset sedam	97	devedeset sedam
78	sedamdeset osam	98	devedeset osam
79	sedamdeset devet	99	devedeset devet
80	osamdeset	100	sto

105	sto pet	2,000	dve hiljade
200	dvesta	3,000	tri hiljade
300	trista	4,000	četri hiljade
400	četristo	5,000	pet hiljada
500	petsto	6,000	šest hiljada
600	šesto	7,000	sedam hiljada
700	sedamsto	8,000	osam hiljada
800	osamsto	9,000	devet hiljada
900	devetsto	10,000	deset hiljada
1,000	hiljadu		

50,000	pedeset hiljada
100,000	sto hiljada
1,000,000	milion

h = loch/hit   j = yet   š = ship   ž = azure

first	**prvi (-a/-o)**	seventh	**sedmi (-a/-o)**
second	**drugi (-a/-o)**	eighth	**osmi (-a/-o)**
third	**treći (-a/-o)**	ninth	**deveti (-a/-o)**
fourth	**četvrti (-a/-o)**	tenth	**deseti (-a/-o)**
fifth	**peti (-a/-o)**	fifteenth	**petnaesti (-a/-o)**
sixth	**šesti (-a/-o)**	twentieth	**dvadeseti (-a/-o)**

once	**jedanput**
twice	**dvaput; dva puta**
three times	**tri puta**

one-half	**pola**
one-quarter	**četvrt; četvrtina**
three-quarters	**tri četvrti(ne)**
one-third	**trećina**
two-thirds	**dve trećine**

33. OPPOSITES

beginning—end	**početak—kraj**
clean—dirty	**čist—prljav**
comfortable — uncomfortable	**udoban— neudoban**
fertile—barren *land*	**plodna—jalova**
happy—unhappy	**srećan — tužan**
life—death	**život—smrt**
friend—enemy	**prijatelj—neprijatelj**
modern—traditional	**moderan—tradicionalan**
modern—ancient	**savremen—starinski**
open—shut	**otvoren—zatvoren**
wide—narrow	**širok—uzak**
high—low	**visok—nizak**
peace—violence/war	**mir—rat**
polite—rude	**ljubazan—neljubazan**
silence—noise	**tišina—galama**
cheap—expensive	**jeftin—skup**
hot/warm—cold/cool	**vruć—hladan**
health—disease	**zdravlje—bolest**
well—sick	**zdrav—bolestan**
night—day	**noć—dan**
top—bottom	**vrh—dno**
backwards—forwards	**napred—nazad**
back—front	**iza—ispred**
dead—alive	**mrtav—živ**
near—far	**blizu—dalek**
left—right	**levi—desni**
inside—outside	**unutra—spolja**
up—down	**gore—dole**
yes—no	**da—ne**
here—there	**ovde(tu)—onde; tamo**
soft—hard	**mek—tvrd**
easy—difficult	**lak—težak**

h = loch/hit   j = yet   š = ship   ž = azure

quick—slow	**brz—spor**
big—small	**veliki—mali**
old—young	**star—mlad**
tall—short	**visok—nizak**
strong—weak	**jak—slab**
success—failure	**uspeh—neuspeh; poraz**
new—old	**nov—star**
question—answer	**pitanje—odgovor**
safety—danger	**bezbednost—opasnost**
good—bad	**dobar—loš**
true—false	**istinit—lažan**
light—heavy	**lak—težak**
light—darkness	**svetlost—tama; mrak**
well—badly	**dobro—loše**
truth—lie	**istina—laž**

Also Available from Hippocrene...

ALBANIAN-ENGLISH/ENGLISH-ALBANIAN STANDARD DICTIONARY
682 pages • 23,000 entries • 5 x 7 • ISBN 0-7818-0979-7 • $22.50pb

ALBANIAN-ENGLISH/ENGLISH-ALBANIAN DICTIONARY & PHRASEBOOK
186 pages • 2,000 entries • 3³/₄ x 7 • ISBN 0-7818-0793-X • $11.95pb

ALBANIAN-ENGLISH/ENGLISH-ALBANIAN PRACTICAL DICTIONARY
400 pages • 18,000 entries • 4³/₈ x 7 • ISBN 0-7818-0419-1 • $14.95pb

BOSNIAN-ENGLISH/ENGLISH-BOSNIAN CONCISE DICTIONARY
332 pages • 8,500 entries • 4 x 6 • ISBN 0-7818-02768 • $14.95pb

BOSNIAN-ENGLISH/ENGLISH-BOSNIAN DICTIONARY & PHRASEBOOK
171 pages • 1,500 entries • 3³/₄ x 7 • ISBN 0-7818-0596-1 • $11.95pb

BEGINNER'S BULGARIAN
207 pages • 5¹/₂ x 8¹/₂ • ISBN 0-7818-0300-4 • $9.95pb

BEGINNER'S SERBO-CROATIAN
323 pages • 5¹/₂ x 8¹/₂ • ISBN 0-7818-845-6 • $14.95pb

BULGARIAN-ENGLISH/ENGLISH-BULGARIAN PRACTICAL DICTIONARY
323 pages • 8,000 entries • 4¹/₄ x 7 • ISBN 0-87052-145-4 • $14.95pb

CROATIAN-ENGLISH/ENGLISH-CROATIAN DICTIONARY & PHRASEBOOK
200 pages • 4,500 entries • 3³/₄ x 7¹/₂ • ISBN 0-7818-0987-8 • $11.95pb

ROMANIAN-ENGLISH/ENGLISH-ROMANIAN STANDARD DICTIONARY
566 pages • 18,000 entries • 4¹/₄ x 7 • ISBN 0-7818-0444-2 • $17.95pb

ROMANIAN-ENGLISH/ENGLISH-ROMANIAN DICTIONARY & PHRASEBOOK
260 pages • 5,500 entries • 3³/₄ x 7¹/₂ • ISBN 0-7818-0921-5 • $12.95pb

BEGINNER'S ROMANIAN
232 pages • 0-7818-0208-3 • 5¹/₂ x 8¹/₂ • ISBN 0-7818-0208-3 • $7.95pb

SERBIAN-ENGLISH/ENGLISH-SERBIAN DICTIONARY & PHRASEBOOK
215 pages • 4,000 entries • 3³/₄ x 7¹/₂ • ISBN 0-7818-1049-3 • $11.95pb

SERBIAN-ENGLISH/ENGLISH-SERBIAN CONCISE DICTIONARY
394 pages • 7,500 entries • 4 x 6 • ISBN 0-7818-0556-2 • $14.95pb

SERBO-CROATIAN-ENGLISH/ENGLISH-SERBO-CROATIAN PRACTICAL DICTIONARY
400 pages • 24,000 entries • 4³/₈ x 7 • ISBN 0-7818-0445-0 • $16.95pb